THE
PANDEMIC
EFFECT

Chapel of Healing, see page 140

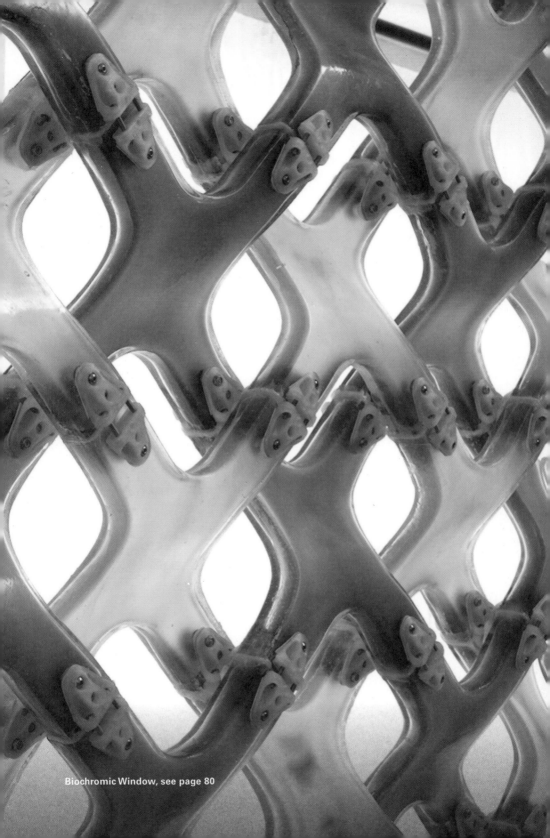

Biochromic Window, see page 80

Nearby Nature, see page 186

Urban Sun, see page 112

Glass Walls, Glass Ceilings, see page 42

Reforestation from Within, see page 74

Natural Healing, see page 182

Redesigning Schools, see page 152

Atelier FCJZ, see page 168

Home.Earth, see page 136

We Need Our Parks, see page 166

Multisensory Wayfinding, see page 150

Quiet Zone, see page 100

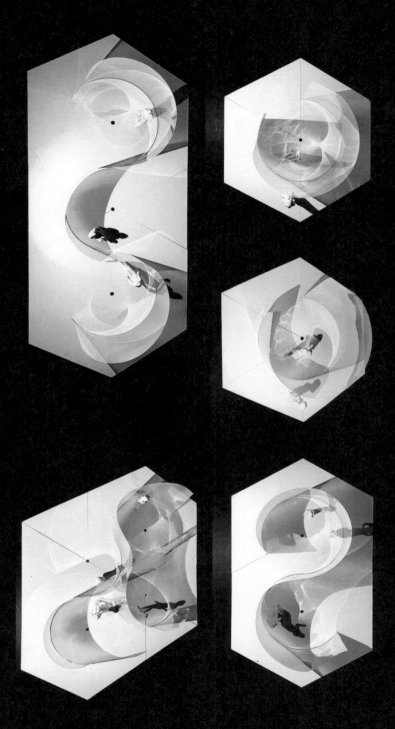

Covid Confessionals, see page 172

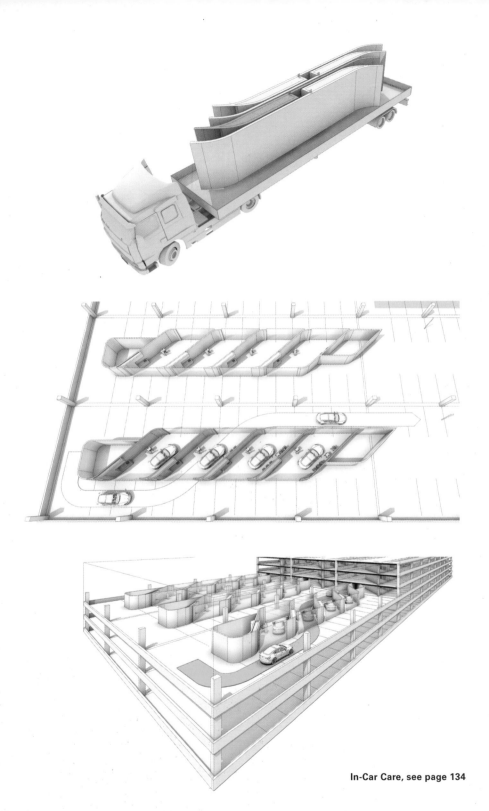

In-Car Care, see page 134

THE PANDEMIC EFFECT

Ninety Experts on Immunizing the Built Environment

BLAINE BROWNELL

Princeton Architectural Press · New York

Contents

This book is dedicated to the memory of Richard Ingersoll, who shaped my understanding of the societal influences of architecture—and to all the others who were victims of the coronavirus pandemic.

Introduction

The novel coronavirus pandemic that emerged in late 2019 resulted in a significant death toll and disrupted human activities worldwide, leading to consequential changes in healthcare, work, retail, school, entertainment, and daily life. The global crisis caused by COVID-19, the illness propagated by the SARS-CoV-2 virus, was not only medical but also existential. In addition to prompting advances in public health, the pandemic motivated reconsiderations of the status quo, resulting in unprecedented shifts in commerce, telecommunications, mobility, policy, employment, education, and culture. Yet, despite a societal upheaval of such magnitude, the ensuing public conversation regarding the coronavirus and its potential solutions has failed to bring adequate attention to a subject of fundamental importance: the built environment.

In the US and similarly industrialized countries, people spend 80–90 percent of their time indoors.[1] When considering the broader built environment—the area developed for human habitation outside of the wild—this figure approaches 100 percent. Physical context plays a significant role in transmitting infectious disease—the cause of approximately one-third of annual deaths worldwide.[2] Yet, there is insufficient awareness about the influences of architecture, infrastructure, and the constructed landscape in spreading illness. Scientists have noted the lack of critical data related to human mobility and interpersonal contacts within the built environment.[3] Beyond isolated laboratory studies of specific physical influences on virus transmission, there is a dearth of analysis regarding the impacts of building attributes and spatial settings of various scales.[4] As the authors of a 2021 National Library of Medicine study argue, "The built environment deserves immediate attention to produce place-specific strategies to prevent the further spread of coronavirus."[5]

Throughout history, when adequate attention has been paid to the influence of constructed spaces on disease, the knowledge has inspired measurable enhancements in buildings and cities. Improvements in sanitation and living conditions, for example, have contributed significantly toward curbing infectious diseases in human populations.[6] In the field of public health, the domain of environmental health emerged in the nineteenth century as the study of the relationships between individual health and the environment.[7] Originally termed the "Sanitary Revolution" based on a series of strategies to control communicable diseases exacerbated by unclean conditions, the environmental health movement inspired proposals to reshape the medical field to address prevention adequately in the twentieth century.[8] The built environment was influenced in-kind: according to Beatriz Colomina, modern architecture developed many of its characteristic qualities in direct response to tuberculosis, "the dominant medical obsession of its time."[9]

Yet despite the measurable improvements sanitation systems have brought to our buildings and cities, a widening gap currently exists between environmental health knowledge and its application. In the built environments of more economically developed countries, comfort and convenience are now prioritized over health. Buildings with inoperable windows ensure indoor temperature and humidity control while shutting out fresh air. Heating, ventilation, and air conditioning (HVAC) systems prioritize establishing an ideal interior climate over eradicating harmful chemicals and pathogens. An emphasis on cost reduction has resulted in the proliferation of cheap building products composed of detrimental synthetic substances. A predisposition against physical exertion privileges elevators and escalators over stairs and ramps. The car is widely preferred for mobility over the bicycle or public transportation. And the most significant example of prioritizing convenience over health is global warming—the deterioration of our planetary climate due to thoughtlessly produced greenhouse gas emissions.

Ironically, the Sanitary Revolution facilitated today's life of convenience by diminishing the threat of environmentally transmitted illness. Widespread hygiene standards in more developed parts of the globe are now taken for granted. And yet, the emphasis on sanitization has gone too far. Chemical disinfectants and antimicrobial coatings have unintentionally led to the emergence of antibiotic-resistant pathogens that pose a severe health threat, particularly in hospitals. Hermetically encapsulated interiors diminish occupant access to fresh air and daylight while increasing the prevalence of sick building syndrome. A dislike for the unruly and unpredictable hazards of wild landscapes has led to the proliferation of the manicured, monocultural lawn.

Considered in the broadest conceptual terms, sanitization has come to shape our general approach to the constructed world. The word *sanitize* has two connotations: "to reduce or eliminate pathogenic agents" and "to make something more acceptable by removing, hiding, or minimizing any unpleasant, undesirable, or unfavorable parts."[10] Not only do human developments seek to eliminate pathogens but also to remove any undesirable elements in the landscape, including all unwanted flora, fauna, and fungi. This treatment is not limited to buildings—even "natural" spaces, such as gardens, parks, and greenways, are controlled, forests are managed, and coastlines are regulated. As the world becomes more urbanized and what is left of wilderness rapidly shrinks, planetary biodiversity is plummeting, soil health is deteriorating, and ecosystems are collapsing. We have, in effect, over-sanitized the globe—and at great peril to our long-term health.

The coronavirus pandemic resulted primarily from the disregard for the built environment's influence on health. Like SARS, bird flu, and Ebola before it, COVID-19 is a disease that emerged from an animal source. Such illnesses result from habitat destruction and biodiversity loss precipitated by human development.[11] As more wild places are invaded and modified, more pathogens are anticipated to cross over from animal to human populations.[12] Once a novel pathogen is established in a human community, the dense configuration of our cities and the interconnectedness of our mobility networks—particularly international air travel—facilitate global transmission. Moreover, as a virus spreads globally via human hosts, the airtight disposition of many buildings and their inadequate airflow and filtration further enhance disease transmission between the hosts and other occupants. Considering how architecture has changed over the last two centuries, today's built environment represents a success in implementing hygiene as a part-to-whole, or inside-out approach—but a failure in the broader establishment of environmental health as a whole-to-part, or outside-in phenomenon.

Unfortunately, the public health sciences have not adequately addressed this failure. Despite the significance of the environment on human health, this subdomain comprises only a tiny portion of the broad spectrum of determinants of health that includes medical care, individual behavior, social circumstances, and genetics and biology.[13] A recent comprehensive review of leading public health sources indicates that the environment is believed to account for only seven percent, or the smallest impact, of all health determinants.[14] This insufficient attention is reflected in higher education, where the number of degrees conferred to environmental sciences has declined relative to other areas of public health, such as health policy and management.[15]

Nevertheless, the definition of environmental factors is now expanding to include a broader set of influences. According to the National Academy of Sciences, "In contrast with traditional environmental health approaches that focus primarily on toxic substances in air, water, and soil, this more recent approach conceptualizes the environment more broadly to encompass a range of human-made physical and social features that are affected by public policy."[16] As a result, decision-makers have begun to recognize the health implications of built environment influences not previously considered in health policy.[17] As a recent National Institutes of Health report argues: "It's time to consider the causes of the causes."[18]

The COVID-19 pandemic has brought new urgency to the imperative that we advance our understanding of the built environment's role in ensuring public health. The idea for this book originated as a way to catalyze the creation and sharing of this knowledge. Since the time of the coronavirus's initial foothold on human society, experts in architecture, engineering, medicine, and other fields have been investigating myriad topics related to COVID-19 and the ways to understand and control this disease and future pandemics. However, before this book's publication, this content had not yet been collected into a single knowledge base.

The Pandemic Effect aggregates the ideas of ninety of the world's leading architects, landscape architects, designers, engineers, materials scientists, and public health experts—creating an expansive overview of insights, arguments, and strategies pertaining to the built environment's relationship to communicable disease. Each entry is concise—a short-form article inspired by the "letters" model in journal publishing. Letters are, according to one definition, "short articles that report results whose immediate availability to the scientific community is deemed important."[19] In this case, the essays are written for the broader public. As the world continues to grapple with the debilitating effects of a multiyear pandemic, the need for immediate sharing is clear. Accordingly, the contributions contained herein are brief and to the point, each communicating a key idea and its supporting rationale in a quickly digestible format. In some cases, the entries represent the seeds of future projects; in others, they serve as snapshots of existing research. In such instances, each author and project is referenced for further study.

The book's content is organized into five chapters. *Histories* offers an overview of past pandemics, technological and social responses, the insights of prior architectural approaches, and strategies for commemoration. *Inside/Outside* addresses the roles of building envelopes and mechanical systems in improving indoor environmental quality and harnessing the benefits of living systems. *Interventions* consists of contemporary methods for direct prevention and control as well as adaptation strategies for postpandemic spaces. *New Strategies* highlights problems in conventional architectural approaches and proposes various design alterations based on pandemic-influenced social transformations. Examples include new workplaces, residential designs, schools, event spaces, and medical delivery methods. Finally, *The Public Realm* considers the broader urban and exurban landscape and related social questions, including new schemes for urban design, mobility infrastructure, streets, parks, gardens, and urban furniture. Together, the contributions represent a broad, albeit incomplete, spectrum of opportunities to rethink the built environment in response to COVID-19.

In the future, architecture has the potential to be a cure—not a cause—of communicable illness. Immunization is defined as the process to make an organism "resistant to a disease or pathogenic agent," or more generally to "provide with protection against or immunity from something."[20] Although the term typically refers to the organisms themselves, immunization might be conceptually applied at a larger scale—to describe the process of protecting human communities, or by extension, the built environment as a whole. The Sanitary Revolution and establishment of hygienic spaces have effectively reduced episodic pathogen transmission, but the coronavirus has revealed significant systemic failures in buildings' and cities' capabilities to protect against the spread of illness. If inoculation is the process whereby a pathogen is introduced to encourage the formation of new protections (antibodies), we might adopt the mindset that the built environment is now inoculated against SARS-CoV-2. The many astute, inventive, and pragmatic offerings included in the following pages represent architecture's new defenses in the battle against infectious disease—and strategies for creating a healthier constructed world.

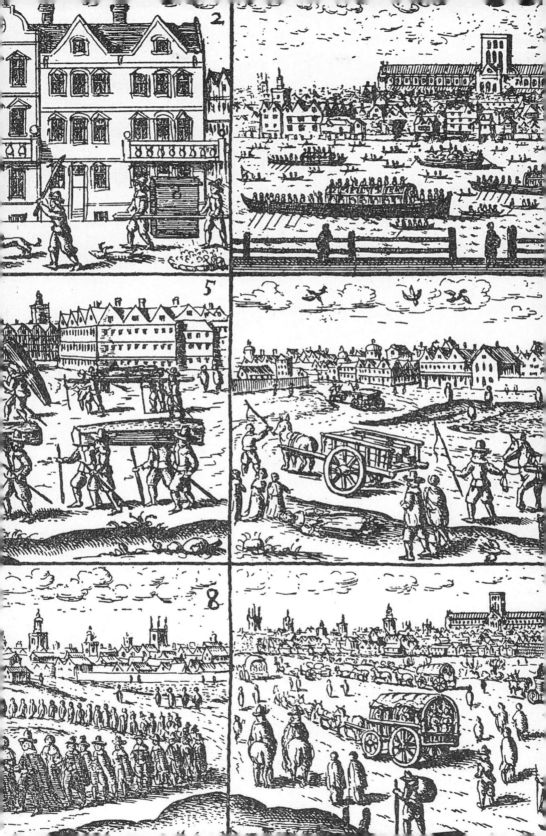

Chapter One

HISTORIES

Past responses to
pandemics and the
reconsideration
of traditional design
approaches

P andemics are not a new phenomenon. The history of pandemics parallels the history of human civilization. Since the plague of Justinian (541–543 CE), there have been at least eighteen recorded pandemics.[1] Defined as infectious outbreaks that grow to encompass an expansive territory, pandemics emerged with the transition from hunter-gatherer to agricultural communities and the growing frequency of human-animal interactions.[2]

A *pandemic* is essentially the unexpected spread of illness at the most significant geographic scale. These factors distinguish it from an *endemic* condition, a predictable occurrence; an *outbreak*, a disease that grows beyond endemic levels; and an *epidemic,* an outbreak that expands to a regional scale.[3] Pandemics are defined not only by their geographic reach but also by their episodic nature, with the presumption that the disease is eventually quelled. Perhaps surprisingly, malaria and tuberculosis are not considered pandemic illnesses because they remain unassailable, even though they cause millions of deaths annually around the globe.[4] Regardless of terminology, this book focuses on the built environment's historic role in spreading diseases of significant concern.

Pandemics have been influenced by the growth of cities and mobility networks. With denser and larger populations, increasing urban development and expansion have made human communities more susceptible to disease emergence and transmission. Notably, nearly half of global pandemics thus far occurred during the nineteenth century, when massive changes were taking place in industrialization and urbanization.[5] The root of the problem concerns the relationship between a disease vector and the human activities and spaces that encourage its transmission. A disease vector is a living agent that transfers a pathogen from an infectious organism to another organism—a typical example of which is the *Anopheles* mosquito, the vector for malaria and other viruses.

The study of disease involves the identification of the vector, the pathogen, and the original conditions for transmission. The pathogens we know may have existed for millions of years before humans created the necessary circumstances for them to cause the first outbreak. Such is the case with malaria, which evolved in primates in Central Africa and was transmitted to human populations that first encroached on their habitats up to ten thousand years ago.[6] After malaria became an epidemic, the mosquito vector and the pathogen remained mysteries for millennia, allowing the widespread expansion of the illness. However, it was eventually recognized that dense human settlements and standing water created ideal conditions for the virus to spread. Like other formidable diseases, malaria has thrived upon three fundamental factors of human-manipulated environments: the expanding encroachment on wilderness (the source of the disease), the proximity and interactions of individuals (the spatial disposition of communities that might encourage spread), and environmental conditions in human settlements conducive for transmission, or vector media (e.g., standing water for mosquito breeding).

These three factors must be considered in the case of any communicable disease: How did the illness originate, and how are our behavior and designed environment influencing its propagation? The sources of many diseases remain unclear today—for example, the Black Death is thought to have originated in East Asia, while cholera may have first developed in India. Regardless of the source, human contact with organisms bearing novel pathogens—which by definition intensifies with the encroachment of human settlements on wilderness—is the standard mechanism of origination.

Regarding transmission, dense communities and transit routes with frequent and long-lasting in-person interactions facilitate spread—although the transmission method varies with the illness (e.g., respiration versus direct contact). Water is a common vector medium—as seen with malaria and cholera—motivating efforts to remove standing water and filter drinking water. Air is also a common vector medium, as seen with smallpox, tuberculosis, and COVID-19, and is inherently more challenging than water to address, given our constant need to breathe. Nevertheless, introducing fresh air and improving airflow—in addition to wearing personal protective equipment (PPE)—are effective methods for lowering transmission rates.

Until the mid-nineteenth century, the microbial sources of infectious diseases remained a mystery. Before that time, human societies nevertheless developed particular behavioral and physical responses to these invisible and unknowable assailants. For example, the miasma theory—the notion that diseases spread via toxic air from decomposing organic matter—was promulgated by Hippocrates in the fourth century BCE, motivating people to avoid rotting vegetation or stagnant environments.[7] Although the inaccurate concept was later replaced by germ theory, developed by chemist Louis Pasteur in 1861, the idea of unhealthy air was not far off the mark. In another example, the practice of quarantine was first introduced in the fourteenth century in Dubrovnik, Croatia, as a way to control the spread of plague via spatial and temporal isolation.[8] Physician John Snow's 1854 discovery of cholera in the contaminated water of London's Broad Street Pump, together with germ theory, led to fundamental changes in urban sanitation practices.[9]

The modernization of architecture and cities that followed was as much a response to this newly recognized enemy, the microscopic pathogen, as it was the product of industrialization. The widening of street networks, development of modern plumbing and sanitary sewer infrastructure, isolation of healing spaces (e.g., asylums and sanatoriums), design of expansive outdoor zones, and widespread adoption of materials representing a hygienic aesthetic (e.g., whitewashed concrete) were all design strategies influenced by germ theory.[10] Today, buildings and cities in many nations still bear many of these hallmarks of the modern architectural response to illness. And yet strategies to isolate and sanitize have gone too far—resulting in the new miasma of "sick" buildings lacking access to fresh air, an overreliance on fallible mechanical systems that can unintentionally intensify the spread of disease, and the homogenization of constructed landscapes that lack the ecological resilience of their more biodiverse predecessors. Adequate preparation for the next pandemic begins with learning where we went wrong.

The following contributions use the lens of history to understand past pandemics, how they have changed the built environment, and what lessons we might have forgotten but can revisit to address today's challenges. Additional topics include cultural changes, such as shifting perspectives about the workplace and the proposal to design a memorial to commemorate the lives lost to COVID-19. Collectively, the contributions reinforce the building's fundamental relationship with illness. As Beatriz Colomina declares in her essay, "All architecture is sick."

Sick Architecture

Beatriz Colomina

Past pandemics reveal the inextricable associations between the built environment and disease.

—

All architecture is sick. Buildings are inseparable from illness. The origin of architecture is the origin of disease. As the doctor Benjamin Ward Richardson stated in *Our Homes and How to Make them Healthy*, a collection of writings by doctors and architects for the 1884 International Health Exhibition in London:

> Man, by a knowledge and skill not possessed by the inferior animals, in building cities, villages, houses, for his protection from the external elements, has produced for himself a series of fatal diseases, which are so closely associated with the productions of his knowledge and skill in building as to stand in the position of effect from cause. *Man in constructing protections from exposure has constructed conditions of disease.*[1]

There is no illness without architecture, and no architecture without illness. Architects and doctors have long engaged in a dance, frequently trading roles, cooperating, influencing one another—even if not always aligned. Furnishings, spaces, buildings, and cities are created by medical emergencies that accrue over centuries. It is easy to forget how these layers have been produced. We treat each pandemic as the first—as if the past is too painful to confront.

Modern architecture emerged amid a medical crisis. Tuberculosis caused millions of deaths worldwide throughout the 1800s and the first half of the twentieth century. Modern buildings provided a defense against this pathogen. The characteristic features of modern architecture, including its uniform whiteness, expansive windows, terraces, and elevation above the ground plane, represented both prevention and antidote. However, society has largely forgotten the connections between modern architecture and tuberculosis.

In these pandemic times, everybody is again thinking about architecture because it is a matter of life and death: distance, hygiene, borders, movements, what is inside and what is outside, who is in and who is out. Suddenly, everybody has become an expert in architecture, redesigning restaurants, schools, universities, and homes. Every space is being precisely adjusted, cleaned, monitored. There has been a massive renovation project with every carpenter, every supply store, furniture manufacturer fully employed. Endless layers of plexiglas have descended onto and into the city. Buildings are even hidden behind these new layers. Entering almost any building is like entering an airport with screening for temperature, identity, and possessions at the door.

Beyond exposing something novel, pandemics reveal what already exists. What COVID-19 has dramatically, even shockingly, made visible is the invisible city—not just the invisible urbanism of hyper-social microorganisms, but the invisible urbanism of inequities, hidden workers, and uneven access to care or empathy. To move forward, we must reflect upon the inextricable ties between architecture and disease. So much that surprises us about the COVID-19 pandemic is not new but has been lying dormant awaiting rediscovery.

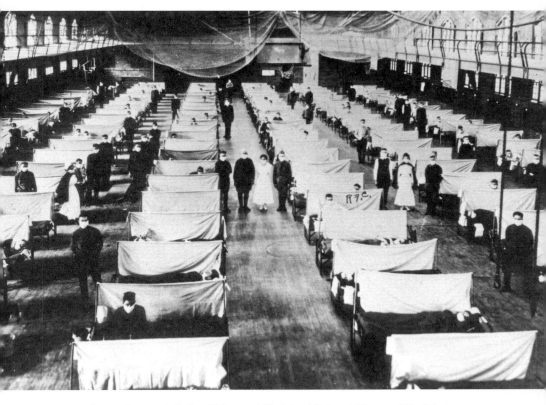

Quarantine ward, National Library of Medicine / National Library of Medicine

*Beatriz Colomina is the Howard Crosby
Butler Professor of the History of
Architecture and the codirector of the
Program in Media and Modernity at
Princeton University.*

The Pneumatic Institution

Jennifer Ferng

An early respiratory-based treatment led to the development of modern gas therapy.

—

The Pneumatic Institution founded by Thomas Beddoes (1760–1808) in 1799 brought a considerably new phenomenon to the public: the medical treatment of gases, or factitious airs, on patients.[12] Located in Bristol, England, this facility aimed to treat tuberculosis patients seeking a cure for their ailments. Through the use of an apparatus developed by Boulton and Watt, Beddoes proposed to undertake scientific investigation and treatment by exploiting respiratory gases in medical practice. Patients were treated by inhaling oxygen and hydrogen. This form of free gas therapy was often given to patients who suffered from diseases thought to be incurable at the time. Some of the patients also suffered from varying forms of paralysis.

James Watt's pneumatic apparatus depicts an alembic, cooling dish, and gasometer drawn in a sectional view—drafted as an illustration for sales literature and patent applications. Materials used to fabricate the gases were mixed in the alembic with a conducting pipe connected to the "refrigerator," where the gas was then cooled. Hydraulic bellows then measured the air and transferred it into the gasometer, where the gas was expelled into an "air-holder" or bag.[13] Such inhalation of gases—desulphurated hydrogen, oxygen, and even carbon dioxide—was thought to promote improvements when patients came down with colds or ulcers. However, Humphry Davy's later development of nitrous oxide or laughing gas highlighted the tragic, if not equally comic, consequences of these treatments.

Supplemental oxygen now provided to COVID-19 patients owes its evolution to the experiments of Beddoes and Watt, who tried to capture the positive attributes of gases for the benefit of their patients. While their treatments did not cure tuberculosis or cancer, the inhalation of gases remains a central concept in contemporary medical practice. These apparatuses soon gave way to Beddoes's obsession with filling rooms with airs—"effervescing mixture with vinegar," for example—forecasting our current ICU spaces where interiors are purified and sanitized. Beddoes's occupation of inhaling powders where "they do not excite anything, if the dust comes in moderate volume" paradoxically underscores how COVID-19's airborne attributes must be countered through protective measures.[14] As part of the ongoing COVID-19 pandemic, respiratory acts of inhalation and exhalation continue to dominate our fixation on what we breathe in, where we breathe, and what we breathe out. Masks, face shields, and PPE gear pose as the thresholds between our respiratory systems and viral infections. Oxygen as a stimulant has never been as critical to our livelihood and our respective medical environments as it is now.

Jennifer Ferng is a senior lecturer in architecture and an academic director at the University of Sydney.

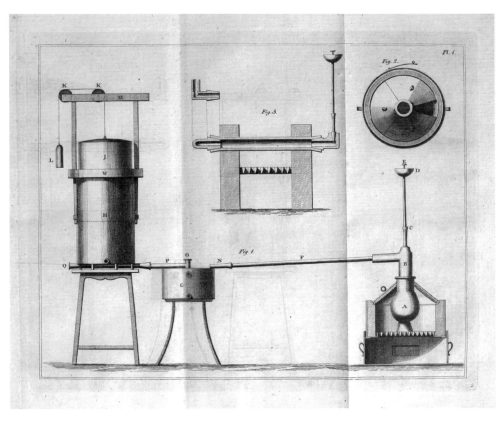

James Watt, *Apparatus for Pneumatic Institution*, 1795. Thomas Beddoes and James Watt,
Considerations on the Medicinal Use and on the Production of Factitious Airs
(Bristol, UK: Bulgin & Rosser, 1795). / James Watt

The Great Acceleration

Thomas Fisher

COVID-19 has ushered in a future of living locally, not globally.

—

Pandemics have profound impacts on the built environment. COVID-19 accelerated preexisting trends and has rebalanced the physical and digital worlds. Today, built space is competing with digital space for everything. When considering a destination, we now ask: "Why would I go? What is the value-added of being physically there?"

The modern profession of architecture emerged in the nineteenth century with the rise of specialized building types. COVID-19 challenged this specialization. Two-thirds of the US economy is now based in people's houses. We now have a tremendous amount of excess built space that sits vacant for large amounts of time. How do we repurpose and reimagine this space? How can we be more efficient in our space utilization?

COVID-19 represents not one but several simultaneous crises: the climate crisis, the Black Lives Matter (BLM) crisis, and the epidemiological crisis. These converging calamities reveal the extent to which the Global North has been playing a Ponzi scheme with the planet—resulting in exaggerated socioeconomic disparities and wildly disproportionate access to resources. We've been borrowing heavily from the future because we've run out of people to exploit. COVID-19 marks the beginning of the end of the Ponzi scheme, which is now collapsing. The events of 2020—the pandemic, BLM marches, and California wildfires—were shots across the bow. The planet was sending warning signs. The next pandemic might be much worse.

What does a post-Ponzi-scheme world look like? This is not a social question; it is a human species question. We have to relate to each other and the planet in profoundly different ways if we are going to survive. We must focus on local materials, renewable energy, and equitable access, and bring an end to one side of the world exploiting the other.

We know how to do this, since humanity dwelled this way for most of our existence. Humans once lived in small tribal communities where we shared viral immunities. One never shook hands with a stranger. Each individual knew at most 100 people, and no clan had more than 150 people. And we constructed shelter using local materials in structures that we either carried with us or recycled when no longer needed. Such an existence may sound primitive, but it was a highly sophisticated life that has much to teach us. A post-Ponzi-scheme world, in other words, may be a twenty-first-century version of the pre-Ponzi-scheme one.

Today, intercontinental air transport and teeming cities have made us highly vulnerable as a species. One possible future is a return to small groups that remain in place, move very slowly, and are connected globally via digital means. There will be a different role for architects, with a focus on recycling, reuse, local foods, and a more flexible use of space. We have accelerated into a future, a lot like our past.

Thomas Fisher is the director of the Minnesota Design Center at the University of Minnesota College of Design.

Gjógv, Eysturoy, Faroe Islands—a remote town that represents a return
to small communities / Annie Spratt

Glass Walls, Glass Ceilings

David Gissen

Those seeking to improve the health of office buildings should consider historic critiques of office environments from the recent past.

—

The sealed, glass-skinned, and now emptied-out office buildings that define office work in many US cities are targeted by critics as emblematic of an unhealthy approach to building. Until recently, architects critiquing these buildings focused on their extracted materials and the intense energy use and carbon embedded in them and their mechanical systems. Today, these buildings' lack of external ventilation and overreliance on recirculated air inspires fear in their workforce. In addition, the potential of increased infections from COVID-19 within such sealed buildings has also inspired further study among architects and engineers into their ventilation systems. As architects explore how to make such interior environments healthier in the future, they might also consider those who explored these issues in the past.

As the historian Michelle Murphy has pointed out, the first studies of the unhealthy air in office buildings occurred long before our contemporary fears: The identification of what would eventually be labeled "sick building syndrome" in the late 1980s and early 1990s was carried out by women working in US office buildings.[15] There, secretarial workers organized and examined the physical impacts on them of the sealed interior spaces within which they worked. Between the 1950s and 1990s, smoking was rampant within US office buildings. Before the widespread use of computation in workplaces, the average secretarial worker would interact with a host of noxious substances—from typewriter correction fluid to chemical xerography. One of the most famous actions addressing sick building syndrome in the US occurred at the offices of the US government's Environmental Protection Agency headquarters. There, Dr. Marsha Coleman-Adebayo sued the US government for ignoring the unique forms of physical danger and harassment she experienced in this workplace.[16] One of her arguments was that sick building syndrome was also caused by harassment of Black women like her and a negligent executive management culture that impacted her health. She won her case.

The environmental feminism and antiracism of the above women are inspiring—and something architects and architecture students might embrace in their explorations of architectural environments and the future design of workplaces. Today, architects and students engaged in environmental questions often struggle to integrate the materialist character of architectural environmentalism with larger questions of human rights or "intersectional" critiques. The above brief example demonstrates that these latter issues are not outside a concern with architectural environments but at the origin point of those critically examining this topic.

David Gissen is a professor of architecture and urban history at the the New School.

Pawel Szvmanski, *Untitled,* **2019** / Pawel Szvmanski

The Nowhere Office

Julia Hobsbawm

COVID-19 has accelerated the demise of our nineteenth-century model of the workplace.

———

I am no architect, but I design spaces in my head. Specifically, I consider the impact physical space has on the headspace that work and the workplace occupy culturally and socially, including the question of how, when, and where we work. What space should "the office" as a fixed space hold in the future of work?

Even before COVID-19, the world of work was messing with our heads, causing the World Health Organization to declare that stress was the health epidemic of the twenty-first century.[17] The office has been epically dysfunctional for years (just search "toxic workplace"), but one thing everyone took for granted was that offices themselves were not a major part of the problem.

That is not quite true, of course. Sick building syndrome has been around for a while, and air quality will clearly be a key legal, safety, and practical issue going forward. But I mean something else. Huge amounts of faith have been put into corporate office space as a gigantic piece of virtue signaling for hundreds of years: offices convey status, power, and intention. I once had an office in London's Somerset House, a vast neoclassical complex. We were up in the eaves of the former Stamp Office, the ultimate palace of eighteenth-century bureaucracy, during the early 2000s, when the office became almost like a fashion accessory: you had to be somewhere cool, or your business or enterprise wasn't cool.

I realized one day that having the most glamorous office in the world wasn't the same as having a functional working space, where the projects, people, and purpose thrived. That wasn't down to the environment only but the work itself. From that day, my operation became hybrid, working partly from fixed spaces and partly from that other place: cyberspace.

Like Le Corbusier before them, postpandemic architects will be redesigning offices not just for clean and safe aesthetics but also for reflecting the point and purpose of a changed and changing set of workers. For people who value mobility and homelife, the office may be more of a stopping-off point than a base.

There is a wonderful scene in Herman Melville's iconic mid-nineteenth-century story of office life, "Bartleby, the Scrivener: A Story of Wall Street," in which the exasperated protagonist, feeling his power slipping, says to his wayward employee: "My mission in this world, Bartleby, is to furnish you with office-room for such period as you may see fit to remain."[18] This now is the question: What remains of the office? The answer is complex, but the simple summary is this: not what it was before.

Julia Hobsbawm is the author of **The Nowhere Office: Reinventing Work and the Workplace of the Future** *(2022) and the founder and copresenter of the podcast* **The Nowhere Office.**

Empty office space in Johannesburg, South Africa / Hennie Stander

Architecture After Simulation

Toyo Ito

The COVID-19 pandemic has intensified society's need to reconnect with nature.
—

Three decades ago, I wrote an essay called "Architecture in a Simulated City." I discussed the search for a suitable space for an ideal life in the computer age. I felt that society was becoming increasingly disconnected from reality and place. I was very interested in how information and computers would change the way we communicate with each other, and I thought that our consciousness would change significantly.

In many ways, the COVID-19 pandemic has accelerated the transition to a computer age that is disconnected from place. We are now in an era where we communicate primarily through digital information, but challenges remain. For example, the Japanese government says it wants 70 percent of its employees to stay home and work online, but the reality is that only 20 percent of employees are working remotely. In my own practice, it is difficult to do architectural design remotely, so everyone comes into the office. Although Zoom has made remote work very convenient, the most effective communication is still face-to-face.

Nevertheless, the pandemic-motivated shift to remote work has reminded me of another early project. The Pao: A Dwelling for the Tokyo Nomad Women was a conceptual design intended to support a new kind of urban dweller. The dwelling provided a bed, a connection to digital media, and places to dress and eat. Ironically, this concept bears similarities to how people have used space during the COVID-19 pandemic. Many individuals have been sequestered in their bedrooms, where they work and take meals, as well as sleep.

I designed the Pao project in the late 1980s when Japan's economy was booming. New restaurants and other venues were being built one after another, and the consumer-based society was very active. One of the reasons I remembered the Pao is this: many Japanese people live in small and cramped housing in urban environments, but they have many fun things to do in the city. However, because people were required to stay at home during the pandemic, their quality of life became very poor. So, as an architect, I feel strongly that housing needs to be more open to nature to create a rich living environment. I also think that public buildings should be designed to remain open and be safe for visitors during a pandemic.

Recently, Tokyo has been experiencing a lot of redevelopment because of the Olympics. The land value is very high, so many tall buildings are built closely together. The result is that human life is separated from nature. As discussed in "Architecture in a Simulated City," our instinctive sensibilities toward place are diminishing. Society has become very homogeneous, and people are less sensitive to the characteristics of a place. Therefore, I think it is vital for architects to help people regain the animal-like sensitivity they have when they are in the midst of nature. Postpandemic architecture should increase connections with nature. One of the ways to do this is to abstract nature and represent it within architecture. Architecture should enable people to choose where they want to live and work freely, just as animals in the wild choose their movements by instinct.

Toyo Ito is the founder of Toyo Ito & Associates, Architects.

Toyo Ito, Sendai Mediatheque, an example of abstracted
nature in architecture, Sendai, Japan, 2000 / Blaine Brownell

Commemorating COVID

Mitchell Joachim, Peder Anker, and Paul D. Miller

A worldwide event as consequential as the COVID-19 pandemic deserves to have a memorial.

———

How can compassionate architects and designers confront our understanding of memorial design in the aftermath of the COVID-19 pandemic? Memorial creation has long served as a conceptual instrument to shape and preserve memory. As abstract monuments, memorials hold a unique position in cultural memory, given their ability to pay tribute to the most challenging periods of human history. As we emerge from a pandemic that has devastated millions of lives, it is essential to contemplate how we should challenge ideas about remembrance and social solidarity on an unprecedented scale.

How must shattered communities conceptualize this stage in global human history? We need to cultivate new tools to remember the precious lives that have been taken. Memory is not a perfect record of the past but a potential filter through which we see tomorrow. We have taken an interdisciplinary approach to investigate global social trauma by revealing techniques from social psychology, history, sustainable architecture, medicine, and music composition.

We have an egalitarian approach to unforgetting the COVID-19 pandemic. Memorial design has a rich history, but the challenges of the twenty-first century require us to develop new strategies for memorialization. Some of the characteristics of this global public health crisis have encouraged many to rethink linear narratives in relation to magnitude and site. Recently, the procedures of abstraction and minimalism have begun to dominate memorial art. From David Adjaye's 2013

Gwangju Pavilion to MASS Design Group's 2018 National Memorial for Peace and Justice, there are innumerable examples of abstract aesthetics being used to aid viewers to think judiciously about the form and function of memorial art. A growing number of contemporary architects and designers have used this style to generate critical questions about the purpose of memorialization. The COVID-19 Memory Research Group aims to scrutinize the architectural and design approaches that are well suited to dynamic narratives, scale, and locality in the aftermath of a global mass-trauma event.

Our current effort began by seeking a universal term. We sensibly selected the word *memoro*. In the international language of Esperanto, the term *memoro* comes from the Latin *memor*, "remembering, mindful." Although the number of active Esperanto speakers is roughly one hundred thousand, the worldwide language has become a symbol of internationalism and cooperation. A memorial planned under the COVID-19 Memory Research Group explores many impartial solutions and neutral paths toward remembrance; thus, our project title, Memoro, must reflect that acutely sensitive position. We believe that solidarity in the aftermath of the pandemic must transcend cultural, social, and national barriers. A global public health crisis necessitates a global response, and research into the memory of COVID-19 must recognize the incredible diversity of experiences that exist when it comes to this abysmal circumstance.

In our latest iteration of the Memoro project, we thought of a multiscaled platform to celebrate remembrance. This working proposal is based on small,

Terreform ONE, rendering of the proposed COVID Memoro / Terreform ONE

elemental distributed artifacts or geometric wedges that can be joined together to form a larger collective monument. Every hand-sized, shard-like element is unique, inscribed with the vital details of an individual who perished because of the virus. Each personal miniature artifact contains a photo, date, location, and audio data file provided by the individual's family and loved ones. Replicas of these personal geometric elements are correspondingly distributed and added to other larger monuments. These aggregate monuments are further assembled into four essential scales of public memorialization; local/community, city/town, regional/national, and continental/global. The aim is to commemorate the memory of everyday people in multiple different levels of tangible engagement. For example, a family can have a piece of the memorial at home and visit the national version that includes a duplicate artifact surrounded by others.

Millions of lives are now gone, but the memories of these precious individuals will assuredly remain with us. The COVID-19 Memory Research Group aims to develop new structures for communities to come together and reflect on the memory of those who perished due to the pandemic. This worldwide crisis was profoundly unfortunate and will not be soon forgotten.

Mitchell Joachim is an architect, the cofounder of Terreform ONE, and an associate professor of practice at New York University.

Peder Anker is a professor of history at the Gallatin School of Individualized Study at New York University.

Paul D. Miller, aka DJ Spooky, is a composer, a multimedia artist, a writer, and a professor at the European Graduate School.

Another Profile

Janette Kim

An eighteenth-century street section drawing reveals lessons for today's increasingly privatized public realm.

—

Shelter-in-place regulations reinforce two despicable narratives: (1) Inside the home, one's survival, triumphs, and failures are attributable to one's merit and grit, and (2) Outside the home, economic productivity and public health are delivered by the enforcement of urban order.[19] These claims deny the collective need for caregiving and universal healthcare.[20] They ignore the absence of protection for essential laborers and the unhoused. And they sacrifice Black lives to enforce property and curfews (even contradicting their own principles to intrude, tragically, into the home of Breonna Taylor).[21] The presumption that the public is out there and the domestic is in here ignores the persistent entanglement of economics, rights, and cultural life across both. Instead, how can we extend public responsibility for collective welfare into the private realm while amplifying political power back out to the city?

To consider this question, I've remasked the section cut of French architect Pierre Patte's 1769 depiction of a city street in *Profil d'une rue* (Profile of a street), to imagine how the edge between the city and the home could reorganize risk, responsibility, and representation. The original drawing depicted the transgression of sewer lines across parcel lines, imprinting the state's responsibility for organizing hygienic and social order directly into the home.[22] This section has already been revised by the privatization of utilities and depleted municipal budgets.[23] But a more effective alteration would reinstate municipal responsibility for clean water as a human right while exposing the system to citizen oversight and the recapture of wastewater and nutrients on-site. In parallel, Patte's drawing sequesters essential workers into the cellar and attic, reinforcing the narrative that survival is a matter of personal responsibility by making caregiving infrastructures invisible. A revised section cut would expand the kitchen and playroom out to the street (or insert the latter into the parlor and nursery). This approach could extend housework into the realm of wage labor while recognizing caregivers' own families as members of an extended household.[24] Thus delineated, the street can take on new meaning, not just as a space for protest against exclusionary practices but as a space of deliberation and governance of common concerns.

Janette Kim is an assistant professor of architecture, the codirector of the Urban Works Agency at California College of the Arts, and a founding principal of All of the Above.

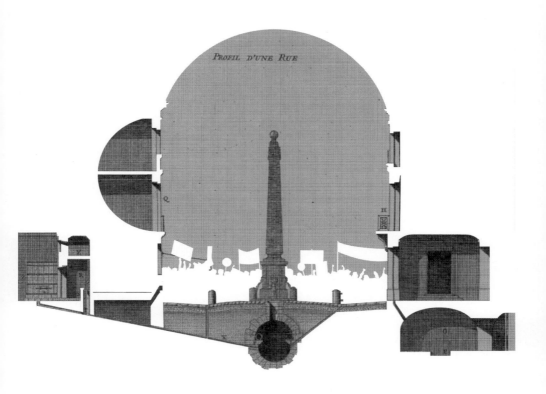

Janette Kim, modified drawing of Pierre Patte's 1769 *Profil d'une rue*, 2022 / Janette Kim

Turning Back
Kengo Kuma

The pandemic prompts a reconsideration of traditional Japanese building techniques.

———

The coronavirus pandemic not only represents a turning point, but also has become a turning-back point for architecture and large cities. The human race has been single-mindedly climbing up a simple slope toward densification over the past two hundred thousand years, putting more distance with time between people and nature. High-rise buildings are the final form of this process of concentration. Although the power of information and communications technology enables people to work in fields and other natural settings without being confined to high-rise buildings, inertia has resulted in cities becoming more concentrated. What the coronavirus pandemic has taught us is that this continued climbing will result in a breakdown of the nature inside of us (our bodies), as well as the nature outside of us (the environment).

Where should the human race turn toward now? I feel that traditional Japanese architecture contains the hint of an answer. Traditional Japanese architecture has a profound aversion to the closing off of spaces and avoids excessive densification. Locally sourced natural materials are used as much as possible. Refined techniques to introduce outdoor ventilation provide a natural air-conditioning system. Space design has evolved to enable space to be flexibly used for various applications rather than being partitioned.

Modernist architecture learned a lot from Japan at the beginning of the twentieth century. Frank Lloyd Wright wrote that he would not have become the person he was if he had not encountered Japan. Ludwig Mies van der Rohe, who was influenced by Wright, came up with the idea to use glass to connect the inside of buildings with the outside. However, the problem of global warming had not emerged at the beginning of the twentieth century, and there was little knowledge about architecture's environmental effects. Modernism perverted transparency as a mere aesthetic and fashion.

The Japanese people realized the danger of the movement toward concentrated urbanization. However, traditional Japanese building techniques were neglected in Japan in the twentieth century, following the US's lead. As a result, the Japanese people themselves forgot about the methods created in Japan. This abandonment of the past resulted in much of the craft being lost and the deterioration of large cities and countryside in Japan.

I want to use the coronavirus pandemic as an opportunity to turn away from the idea of urban concentration. There is so much to be learned by the building traditions of Japan and their inherent connections to nature.

Kengo Kuma is the founder of Kengo Kuma & Associates and professor emeritus in the Department of Architecture at the University of Tokyo.

Veranda of Koto-in, Daitoku-ji, Kyoto, Japan / Blaine Brownell

Quarantine, or the Art of Intermediary Space

Geoff Manaugh & Nicola Twilley

The history of quarantine is the story of architecture and geography.

—

Toward the end of the eighteenth century, the British social reformer John Howard embarked on a series of grand tours across mainland Europe. Rather than visit the standard sights—ancient ruins and famous monuments—Howard set himself a goal of inspecting prisons, jails, and dungeons throughout the continent. Part architecture critic, part humanitarian, he hoped to improve the conditions under which people were detained. In the final years of his travels, however, Howard shifted his focus to quarantine stations: buildings equally devoted to containment, but for reasons of preemptive medical isolation rather than penitence or punishment.

Quarantine is a medical practice in the form of an architectural protocol: it is the deliberate manipulation of space and time for the purpose of controlling epidemic disease. As a tool for public health, quarantine most often works by delaying the arrival of someone or something suspected of infection. If its goal is to prevent two people from exposure to one another, then quarantine is most useful wherever those people are likely to meet. The history of quarantine is thus also a history of cultural encounters—of trade routes, religious pilgrimage, and economic exchange. Through a design vocabulary of waiting rooms and courtyards, verandas and balconies, inspection corridors and windswept arcades, quarantine is an art of the intermediary location or buffer space.

Since its invention in the Adriatic Sea region in response to the Black Death, quarantine has relied on both architecture and geography to establish zones of purity and danger. Even before the advent of modern germ theory, quarantine offered protection through separation, keeping individuals and groups away from one another, in part by pushing quarantine buildings outside city walls and onto well-guarded islands and peninsulas. It is only in our age of advanced air-handling equipment and easily disinfected building materials that quarantine has moved to the center of things, no longer on the periphery but in the very midst of the communities it is meant to protect.

After visiting dozens of quarantine facilities, from Ireland to Italy, Malta to Marseille, Howard designed his own ideal lazaretto. In the resulting plan, all of quarantine's strategies for controlling space-time can be seen. Situated on a windswept peninsula overlooking a bay, Howard's lazaretto included widely separated buildings for disinfecting goods and surveilling ships' crews; gardens, which allowed for self-sufficiency, reducing exposure to the outside world; and even a large metal chain stretched across the harbor to prevent unregulated arrivals and departures. No less importantly, Howard's design introduced space for recreation and pastoral care—an attention to the lived experience of quarantine that has all too often been overlooked. Today, with new and emerging diseases, such as Ebola or COVID-19, the architecture of quarantine is still being fine-tuned, but Howard's lessons have not lost their moral and spatial relevance.

Howard's quarantine travels would ultimately prove to be his last: he died—it is believed after contracting typhus, an infectious disease—while inspecting quarantine facilities in what is now Ukraine.

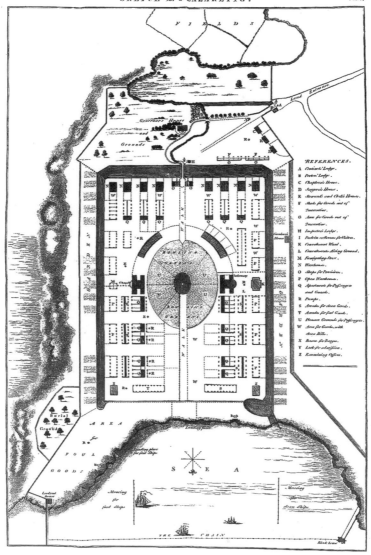

John Howard, *Sketch for a Lazaretto*, 1789, Wellcome Collection,
University of London / John Howard

Geoff Manaugh is the author of A
Burglar's Guide to the City *(2016) and
a frequent contributor to the* Atlantic,
Wired, *the* New York Times Magazine,
and other publications.

*Nicola Twilley is the cohost of
the podcast* Gastropod *and a frequent
contributor to the* New Yorker.

Manaugh and Twilley are coauthors of
Until Proven Safe: The History and
Future of Quarantine *(2021).*

Disease and the City

Deyan Sudjic

History shows how cities have been shaped in response to past pandemics.
—

In what we are shamefully prepared to call a normal year, the world suffers around 1.4 million tuberculosis deaths, mostly in India, Indonesia, and China. Malaria kills fewer people but still accounts for five hundred deaths annually. In the Global North, it took the pandemic to force those of us who live insulated by clean water, antibiotics, and climate to think again about the intimate connections between health, the city, and architecture in a way we haven't for a century.

Cholera is less lethal than the plagues that killed up to a third of the population of Europe in the Middle Ages but was a recurring curse throughout the nineteenth century. It was particularly dangerous in the exploding big cities. Paris was badly hit in 1832, with one-fifth of the one hundred thousand cholera deaths across France that year, and again in 1849, when nineteen thousand people died in the capital.

It is often claimed that Baron Georges-Eugène Haussmann's regularization of Paris's medieval street plan was part of a strategy to make the place less vulnerable to revolutionary mobs. Civil disorder was an issue. Napoleon III was also determined to glorify himself by building a grandiose capital city. But underneath those new boulevards, Haussmann's engineers dug an elaborate network of sewers to neutralize the threat of cholera.

In Italy, malaria was a determining factor in the shape of urban development from the time of the draining of the marshes around Rome during the Mussolini era. Then, as now, there were plenty of conspiracy theorists claiming that the mainstream scientists had got it all wrong and that malaria, as its name suggests, was a sickness caused by bad air, not by mosquitoes.

Like Alvar Aalto's tuberculosis sanatorium in Finland, Josef Hoffman's outside of Vienna was an icon of early twentieth-century architecture. Indeed it's possible to read hygiene as the single idea that runs throughout the modern movement. Le Corbusier was obsessed with it. In *Vers un Architecture* (Toward an Architecture), he wrote,

> Demand a bathroom looking south…
> Never undress in your bedroom…
> Demand one really large living room…
> Demand bare walls…
> Demand concealed or diffused lighting…
> Demand ventilating panes to the windows in every room.[25]

With Perspex screens at every shop counter, and crews of workers scrubbing trams, buses, and trains every hour, these demands don't seem quite so eccentric now.

As we emerge from the COVID-19 threat, we should take the opportunity to learn from the history of modernism and better understand the modern movement's motivations and origins—and, more importantly, to learn not to repeat its assault on the essential qualities of urban life, potentially the most pernicious outcome of the pandemic.

Deyan Sudjic is a writer and director, the former director of the Design Museum, London, and an editor of **Domus.**

Le Corbusier, interior view of bathroom, Villa Savoye, Poissy, France, 1929 / Blaine Brownell

Chapter Two

INSIDE / OUTSIDE

Interior-exterior relationships and the influence of indoor environmental quality on human health

Buildings are designed to offer protection. However, in the case of the coronavirus pandemic, many buildings did the opposite. A fundamental problem is air quality, which is typically worse inside buildings than outside, particularly in the case of viruses. SARS-CoV-2, the virus causing COVID-19, is spread via airborne droplets of varying sizes and is transmitted from a host individual to potential recipients. The fine droplets remain suspended in the air and accumulate within interior environments.[1] Indoors, these particles can pose a threat for hours after a host has left a space. For this reason, the US EPA has identified "being indoors rather than outdoors, particularly in indoor environments where ventilation with outside air is inadequate" as the first circumstance likely to increase the risk of infection.[2]

The inadequacy of indoor ventilation is generally a modern-day problem. With the development and proliferation of air-conditioning technology in the twentieth century, building envelopes were made less permeable by design. The logic seemed straightforward: the less air exchanged between inside and outside, the greater control over indoor temperature and humidity. As a result, it is now standard practice for most non-residential buildings to have inoperable windows. However, this hermetic isolation works against the imperative for human respiratory health. Long before the coronavirus pandemic, the unhealthy air in modern buildings was blamed for a number of occupant ailments that are now collectively termed sick building syndrome. COVID-19 merely compounded the problem. The effective aerosol transmission of the SARS-CoV-2 virus in poorly ventilated spaces reinforces the hazards of inoperable building enclosures.

Once buildings are sealed off from the outdoors, fresh air must be introduced via other means. Air delivery is one of the functions of HVAC systems, which also condition, filter, and recirculate indoor air. Unfortunately, typical mechanically assisted airflow provides inadequate protection against chemical or microbial exposure. For example, recent studies of the indoor aerosol transmission of the SARS-CoV-2 virus have shown that conventional HVAC systems provide insufficient protection for occupants.[3]

Air quality is even more concerning in the case of air-conditioning, which optimally functions in recirculation mode—not as a source of ventilation.[4] Scientific studies have determined that air-conditioned spaces increase infection risk, with virus transmission between four and nineteen times more likely to occur in such areas than in outdoor spaces.[5] For this reason, air-conditioning has been identified as a COVID-19 "superspreader."[6] Filtration is used in the absence of fresh-air intake, but typical filters are not a substitute for ventilation and source control.[7]

The separation of the indoors from the outside world brings additional challenges. For example, air-conditioning contributes measurably to the climate crisis. In addition to being a significant source of CO_2 emissions, air-conditioners are anticipated to increase fourfold in quantity by 2050 due to global warming.[8] Inoperable facades require occupants to utilize air-conditioning even on days with mild temperatures because there is inadequate ventilation to combat solar heat gain— thus exacerbating the problem.

Air-conditioners can also harbor pathogens that are recirculated in stale indoor air. Conventional chemical disinfectants and antimicrobial coatings—used in full force during the pandemic—are seen as a solution. However, these substances have fatal flaws: one is adverse health effects in occupants, and another is the development of antimicrobial-resistant "superbugs" that represent a worsening public health challenge— particularly in healthcare settings.[9] Yet another problem is that these chemicals deplete the beneficial bacteria in a space that might otherwise combat pathogens.

The contributions in this chapter address the human and environmental health challenges presented by contemporary building envelopes and mechanical systems and how they might be redesigned to optimize indoor environmental quality. Additional considerations include the interior cultivation of living systems, including oxygenating plants and beneficial microbiota, typically relegated to the outdoors.

Open Architecture

Dorit Aviv

We can overcome the fraught relationship between health and energy savings by restoring natural ventilation systems.

When reimagining a resilient built environment for the post-COVID-19 era, we must tackle two entangled global environmental crises, not only the health crisis brought about by the pandemic but also that of climate change. During the pandemic, buildings became the sites of the rapid spread of the SARS-CoV-2 virus. Indoor environments, with a limited supply of fresh air, became fertile grounds for aerosol transmission. As a result, many buildings closed their doors and shut down. Those that remained open saw sharp surges in energy consumption due to increased indoor ventilation rates, creating a substantial additional load on buildings' mechanical systems. Eliminating air recirculation and increasing fresh-air intake often resulted in a 200 percent spike in energy demand.[10] The pandemic stresses a recurring question in architectural system design: How can a building's infrastructure provide adequate ventilation to maintain public health while avoiding energy surges fueled by our overreliance on carbon-intensive technologies?

This fraught relationship between health and energy savings is not new. Measures taken to improve buildings' efficiency after the 1970s energy crisis, which included the design of airtight envelopes and limited delivery of fresh air through the recirculation of already heated or cooled air, resulted in poorly ventilated interiors and the sickening of building occupants, otherwise known as sick building syndrome.[11]

Throughout the pandemic, the outdoor environment, with its unlimited supply of fresh air, offered a safe alternative for many activities, especially during the warmer months of the year. Yet as the pandemic raged across many parts of the globe, another health hazard, a heat wave on the order of a one-in-a-thousand-year weather event, resulted in hundreds of heat-stress casualties within a few days in the North American West.[12] Purchases of air-conditioners spiked, as did electricity demand and subsequent power outages, as people scrambled to find a remedy for the heat. The building infrastructure failed to provide a safe thermal shelter in such crucial moments.

We are trapped in a vicious cycle. Greenhouse gas emissions contribute to the planet's warming, leading to an increased need for cooling, but more cooling leads to more emissions. Unless emissions are drastically curbed, these extreme summer temperatures will no longer be an anomaly but become the norm, causing major health risks globally. Importantly, however, cutting down on energy consumption cannot come at the expense of proper ventilation in buildings.

The current paradigm for building indoor ventilation and temperature control is failing. Architects and engineers design buildings as closed environments: the interior is separated from the outdoor climate through sealed facades. Many buildings have inoperable windows in order to manage interior environments mechanically. Interior climate and ventilation controls rely on fan-power and energy-intensive refrigeration systems. The mechanical cooling systems in these buildings then eject all the heat taken from the interior space directly to the urban exterior, contributing to the heat-island effect in already broiling cities.

We need a new model in which increased ventilation and energy conservation work hand in hand. The first step is to restore natural ventilation to buildings where possible. Natural ventilation can improve air quality and cooling in many climatic regions and seasons. However, when outdoor temperatures rise beyond a certain threshold, natural ventilation may not provide enough cooling to keep people safe, and additional steps must be taken to prevent heat stress. Architectural solutions, such as shaded facades and thermal mass, can help reduce heat gain and dampen indoor-temperature peaks.

In cases where these measures still do not provide safe temperature ranges, active low-energy solutions can also provide much-needed cooling. Radiant cooling is one such solution. It relies on chilled water tubes embedded in floors, walls, or ceilings and provides cooling at a much lower carbon footprint than air-conditioning.[13] Since radiant systems do not control the air temperature and instead work through a building's surfaces, they can be coupled with natural ventilation to supply fresh air without increasing energy consumption.[14] However, unlike central air systems, which are designed to be hidden in mechanical rooms and plenum spaces, these solutions are part of the building's exposed surfaces. They, therefore, rely on architectural design taking an active role in how air and heat move through the buildings.[15]

Facades, floors, and walls can all be active components in tuning the interior climate and channeling airflow through the building. Yet architects have taken a back seat on designing for climate for more than fifty years. If we are to rise to the global challenges faced by our cities and buildings and make them resilient to future pandemics, we need to move toward an open architecture, where the outdoor environment is harnessed to provide ample fresh air—an architecture in which public health and building energy efficiency are no longer at odds with one another, in which building surfaces and openings are recentered in their capacity to deliver and channel ventilation and heat, and in which equitable cooling solutions and clean air are accessible to all.

Dorit Aviv is an assistant professor at the Weitzman School of Design and the director of the Thermal Architecture Lab at the University of Pennsylvania.

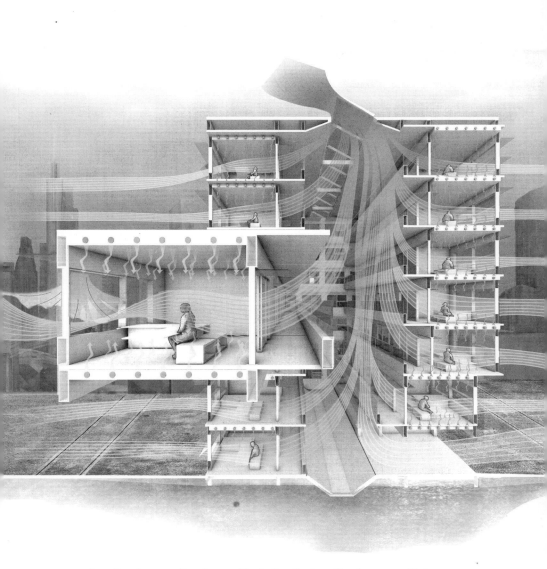

A sectional perspective diagram illustrating the benefits of cross ventilation and thermally conditioned architectural surfaces / Dorit Aviv

Windows Determine Our Situation

Daniel A. Barber

Windows' operability is a fundamental condition of human health and welfare.
—

I refer to media theorist Friedrich Kittler's key statement that "Media determines our situation" when I ask, "Do windows determine our situation?"[16] How do we open windows, screen them, or filter them? Windows improve life; they are a visible trace of energy use and systems technology—or its absence.

Windows determine our situation. Do you have cross ventilation? Can you keep your home, workspace, or space of leisure ventilated? One of the central questions of the pandemic, and pandemics to follow, will be this: "Can you open your window?" The sealed hotel room or office should be abolished. All windows need to open. This capability provides a salve to the six-foot-distance rules and the persistence of mask wearing: keep the windows open and the air flowing.

Window inoperability also defines the entanglement between COVID-19 and climate change—both politicize the built interior in new ways. As I write this in January 2022, while the Omicron variant rages through the US and the world, teenagers are walking out of schools that they deem unsafe. Conditions in the interior of buildings threaten the body politic. In this case, opening the window is likely not enough. New ventilation systems, fans, and targeted openings must keep air flowing.

The classroom, the office, the hospital, and spaces of leisure and consumption all require a different sort of air-conditioning after Covid: moving and cleaning the air while taking advantage of this opportunity to experiment in related carbon-reduction practices. Think about insulation, for example. Consider the dynamics between summer and winter conditions: Are there ways to collect solar radiation? What are the opportunities within the building for retrofit, efficiency, and, often at the scale of schools or institutions, energy generation—energy oases as spaces of generation and efficiency?

Opening the window is the key. Opening the window determines our situation. Let the air flow.

Windows are media. The windows depicted here are from the castle in Heidelberg, Germany, on a bright summer day. They have a physical, leaded presence, a rich absorption of solar rays, and a contrast with the gleaming stone. They are windows that shed light, that bring life. Windows as screens on which we read the history of thermal conditions, thermal decisions, and the adaptive capacities of buildings and bodies, systems, and physiologies, to be climate changed.

Daniel A. Barber is a professor of architecture at the University of Technology Sydney (UTS).

Detail of the Heidelberg Castle facade, Heidelberg, Germany / Daniel A. Barber

Alive

David Benjamin

The microbiome of buildings can support the collective health of building occupants.

—

Microbes are everywhere. Invisible to the human eye, they live in the air, within the walls, and on every surface. We have always lived together with microbes, and most of them contribute to our well-being.

The human body has more microbial cells than human cells. Although a few types of bacteria and viruses make us sick, many others defend us and limit the effects of the harmful ones. Bacteria in the gut release chemicals that affect mental health. Viral DNA helps us process and store memories. From this perspective, each of us is a metropolis teeming with life. Microbes make us who we are.

As you read this text, you will shed two million bacteria, breathing them out and shedding them from your skin and hair. Most of them will die. And the ones that survive in typical architectural environments tend to be the most dangerous to humans. Yet, in settings with a diverse community of microbes, the harmful organisms are outweighed by the benign ones.

What if we created architectural environments to host a diversity of microbes? Architecture could include spaces for both humans and microorganisms. Rooms could have different microclimates for different types of microbes. Microbial reservoirs could supplement equipment for ventilation, heating, and cooling. Materials could be sponges with infinite surface areas. A bioreceptive material like loofah could support microbes with cavities of different sizes and shapes that provide different levels of temperature, moisture, and airflow. Walls become clouds to nourish humans. Just as a healthy gut microbiome promotes our individual health, a healthy building microbiome promotes our collective health. A new living architecture is born from probiotic buildings.

A holobiont is a collection of different species living symbiotically. The humans, microbes, and other organisms each contribute to the well-being of the whole. We are all made of each other. And all architecture is multispecies architecture. In the future, buildings could be like our skin and gut, with colonies of microbes tuned to promote our health.

Humans are the microbes of the city. For both humans and microbes, diversity is the key to well-being. And to design for diversity is to design for our collective future.

David Benjamin is the founding principal of The Living and an associate professor in the Graduate School of Architecture, Planning and Preservation at Columbia University.

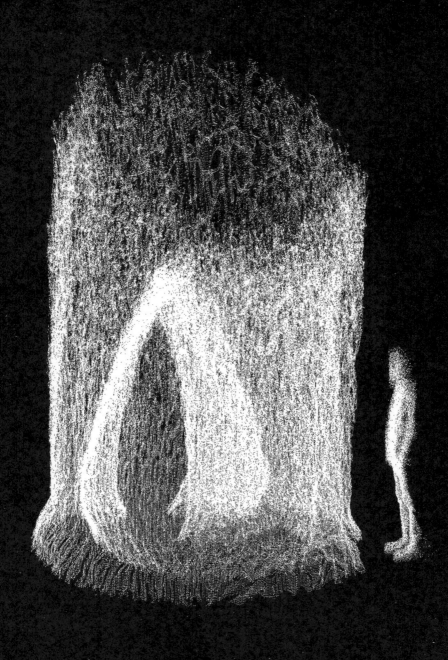

**Simulation of a probiotic environment for the Alive installation at the
Venice Architecture Biennale by The Living, 2021 /** The Living

Optimize Daylight

Emmanuelle Bourlier

Structural honeycomb panels improve indoor environmental quality.

——

An effective architectural strategy to improve both human health and environmental performance began as a purely aesthetic endeavor. The first application of Panelite's ClearShade panel was at the McCormick Tribune Campus Center at the Illinois Institute of Technology (IIT), designed by the Office for Metropolitan Architecture (OMA). Architect Rem Koolhaas had used Panelite's interior panel, composed of a structural honeycomb encapsulated in resin, in several applications and now wanted to use it on the exterior. The initial concept was to bond the honeycomb between two panes of glass, but we eventually decided to employ standard insulated glazing unit (IGU) technology, simplifying both installation and adoption by embedding a new technology inside a known and trusted one. We did a lot of testing to get the tubular honeycomb structure into the IGU, and for IIT, we created a custom bright orange color that was vital to OMA's design.

After construction of the IIT project and as ClearShade was used on other projects, we began to learn about its other technical performance attributes beyond aesthetics. At the Marquis Condominiums in Miami, Arquitectonica specified ClearShade to ensure visual privacy between balconies, taking advantage of angled honeycomb cells to direct lines of sight away from neighbors and toward the skyline. Miami-Dade County requires hurricane-safe glazing, and we learned that the honeycomb insert structurally improved the units' wind resistance, by mitigating deflection of the outer lite under wind loads.

On other projects, clients regularly commented that there was no glare, only beautiful, diffuse daylight. The honeycomb inserts are roughly a half inch deep, and daylight gets bounced within the cells, softening the illumination while maintaining ample daylight levels. (Panelite's interior panels similarly transmit daylight while offering visual privacy.) The honeycomb-cell walls also act like a series of small louvers, blocking the heat of the sun, reducing solar heat gain and accordingly reducing the need for air-conditioning. Other facade solutions, such as shades or electrochromic glazing, are problematic because they reduce daylight during peak hours, requiring the use of artificial lighting and negatively impacting occupant well-being.

We began to study the panels from an environmental performance standpoint. Based on collaborations with Arup and the Lawrence Berkeley National Laboratory, we can now quantify the energy-saving and daylighting performance benefits of ClearShade—including changes caused by varying the cell size, angle, or color of the honeycomb core. We can determine which variables will optimize performance based on a project's site and orientation.

Although user interest in ClearShade was expanding before the COVID-19 pandemic, it has intensified since. The scale of projects is increasing. Occupant well-being was a growing concern prior to COVID-19—as evidenced within the Leadership in Energy and Environmental Design (LEED) and WELL building standards and the work of leading architects—but our clients place a higher priority on user well-being now. Occupant health has become a more significant concern, and companies are trying to

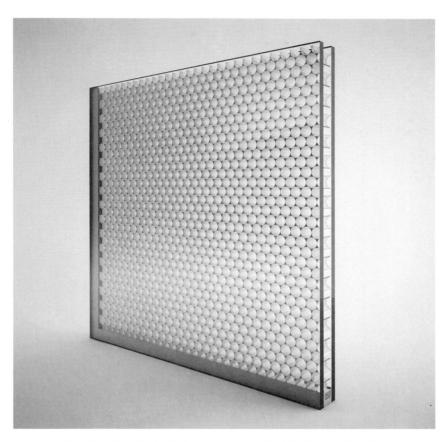

Panelite, ClearShade glazing unit for optimized daylighting / Panelite

attract people back to the workplace. Current applications for ClearShade include offices, transportation hubs, hospitals, and schools—there's such a strong connection between daylight and the ability to learn and process information.

Despite its tragic consequences, the pandemic seems to have positively amplified a growing awareness of the health benefits of daylight in our built environment, benefits that are now being scientifically measured but have always been intuitively felt. When you go to these all-day indoor conferences lit only by artificial light, you feel sick at the end of the day. We can do much better. This is Panelite's future: providing amply daylight spaces that give people a sense of well-being while optimizing energy savings.

Emmanuelle Bourlier is the founding partner and chief executive officer of Panelite.

Beyond Dilution

Andrew Cruse

Buildings should be designed to adaptive thermal-comfort standards instead of a traditional, resource-intensive mechanical-systems approach.

—

COVID-19 makes us decidedly uncomfortable in the very indoor environments that we design to be comfortable. In doing so, it highlights longstanding connections between architectural comfort, health, and energy use. For example, a typical architectural response to the virus has been to increase indoor ventilation. We dilute our discomfort with more outdoor air brought in with mechanical systems and through open windows. Yet such solutions risk creating other types of discomfort—thermal and acoustic—as well as using greater amounts of energy to condition greater quantities of outdoor air. We can find a more robust architectural approach to the challenges of COVID-19 in the adaptive thermal-comfort model. This model creates connections between indoor and outdoor climates that are fundamental to a building's organization.[17] Architects are ideally suited to imagine how the ideas of adaptive thermal comfort can be part of an overall design to create more comfortable, healthy, and energy-efficient buildings.

Mixed-mode buildings, which integrate air-conditioning and natural ventilation, are the architectural corollary to adaptive thermal comfort ideas.[18] They combine air-conditioning and natural ventilation in different arrangements. The variety of comfort conditions found in mixed-mode projects contrasts with the one-size-fits-all comfort model of sealed and air-conditioned buildings, the very buildings in which the virus can thrive. Although the architectural press seldom highlights mixed-mode techniques per se, we can find them in the work of established practices and younger firms, whose projects combine indoor and outdoor climates in poetic and performative ways. Lacaton & Vassal achieve this with nested organizations and seasonal changes from their Maison Latapie (1993) in Bordeaux, France, to the more recent eighteen housing units in Rixheim, France. SANAA does it with a focus on transparency and landscape, as seen in the Grace Farms project (2015) in New Canaan, Connecticut. Innovative engineering practices, such as Transsolar, Arup, and Atelier Ten, consistently collaborate with architectural practices on mixed-mode projects—an example of which is the WA Museum Boola Bardip (2020), in Perth, Australia, where Atelier Ten collaborated with OMA and local architect Hassell. What characterizes this work is a desire to create bespoke comforts that combine indoor and outdoor climates in ways that integrate with the project's spatial, temporal, and material organization.[19]

Considering Covid in the context of comfort helps architects think beyond dilution to find ways that architectural design can provide at least partial answers to challenges posed by the pandemic. As our attitudes shift from trying to eliminate the virus to learning to live with it, design strategies that celebrate the entanglements of comfort, health, and energy make such an approach all the more vital.

Andrew Cruse is an associate professor of architecture in the Knowlton School of Architecture at the Ohio State University

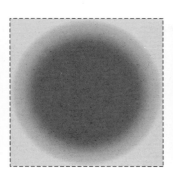  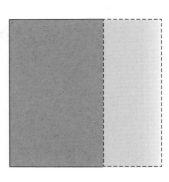

Concurrent Mixed Mode
Buildings with both air conditioning and natural ventilation in the same space that can be used simultaneously. Occupants regulate what mode is used and when.

Changeover Mixed Mode
Buildings with both air conditioning and natural ventilation in the same space. The building changes between these modes, typically on a seasonal basis.

Zoned Mixed Mode
Buildings with dedicated air conditioning in some spaces and natural ventilation in others. Occupants can move from climate to climate within the same building.

Thermal diagrams showing how mixed-mode buildings combine air-conditioning and natural ventilation in different spatial and temporal arrangements. / Andrew Cruse

Reforestation from Within

Jefferson Ellinger, Jason Vollen, Matthew Gindlesparger, and Anna Dyson

A wall of air-purifying hydroponic plant pods exhibits potential pathogen-reducing capabilities.

—

We originally developed the Active Modular Phytoremediation System (AMPS), a wall of air-purifying hydroponic plant pods, to address deteriorating indoor air quality from within buildings rather than rely solely on the filtration of outdoor air. With the emergence of the coronavirus pandemic, the system has also shown promise to reduce the concentrations of viral loads within building environments.

To address potential viral concentrations, AMPS processes indoor air, passing it through an enhanced biological filtration media, replacing the return-air filter as a stand-alone system that filters the local airstream. Rather than filtering the airstream solely with activated carbon or high efficiency particulate air (HEPA) filters that sterilize it by removing virtually all particles, this system leverages biological capacities to create a healthier airstream for the building and its occupants. Bio-based air filtration introduces a wide variety of healthy microbiota that occur naturally with the plant rhizosphere into the airstream while also filtering out the most harmful particulates and pollutants. Additionally, the system reduces the concentration of carbon dioxide, creating a more oxygen-rich environment. By introducing healthy microorganisms into the building airstream, the biodiversity found within the built environment radically changes to one more similar to the biodiversity found in nature.

Whereas traditional techniques sterilize the filtered air of a building, human pathogens tend to dominate, as they are the microorganisms most readily transported by the humans using the facility. In contrast, AMPS creates an environment where biodiversity is reestablished, effectively reducing the concentration of human pathogens and increasing the levels of healthy microorganisms. Furthermore, our studies show that occupants exposed to the AMPS-filtered air have exhibited improved factors, indicating an environment beneficial to human health.

Based on pandemic-related concerns about air quality related to the spread of a viral pathogen, lab testing is currently underway to determine the system's efficacy against the coronavirus. Our hypothesis is that AMPS's benefit to occupants is substantial because the plants filter airborne viral particles and increase the biodiversity of the environmental microbiome. Furthermore, we designed the latest iteration of AMPS to bring the plants and filtration together in a single room without the need for a direct connection to the building ventilation system. Deploying plants and air filtration together at a large enough scale to have a measurable impact is a complex endeavor due to the intricate biological processes of the plants. For example, potted plants alone could not improve the airstream to necessary levels. However, when the active filtration system is appropriately scaled and tuned to fit a space, the benefits of increased biodiversity and reduced carbon-dioxide concentration may be achieved, creating a healthy airstream for the occupants while minimizing the impacts of the spread of the coronavirus.

Prototype of the Active Modular Phytoremediation System, version 2, with air-purifying hydroponic plant pods / Matthew Gindlesparger

Jefferson Ellinger is an associate professor in the School of Architecture at the University of North Carolina at Charlotte and a partner of Fresh Air Building Systems.

Jason Vollen is a principal at AECOM and a partner at Fresh Air Building Systems.

Matthew Gindlesparger is an architect, a certified passive house consultant, and a partner at Fresh Air Building Systems.

Anna Dyson is the Hines Professor of Sustainable Architectural Design and a professor at the Yale University School of the Environment and a partner at Fresh Air Building Systems.

Porch Practice

Charlie Hailey

The pandemic renewed the porch's critical social and environmental roles.

—

Before the pandemic, porches languished with our preference for the indoors and conditioned air. Most North Americans spent less than 7 percent of their day outside, where porches lingered as real estate amenities, more about a nostalgic idea and image than an occupiable domestic space, and served as oversized mailboxes on which video doorbells kept watch for porch pirates. But with the onset of COVID-19, many rediscovered porches along with other open-air spaces at building edges. Porches became stages to perform, outdoor rooms to breathe fresh air without breaking quarantine, and places to see and be seen and to talk and exchange news about the pandemic. Impromptu opera arias, jazz jam sessions, and poetry readings entertained neighborhoods, as residents momentarily forgot illness and separation to remember connections with nature and people.

During the pandemic, the porch became a method that recalls the work of architects Alison and Peter Smithson: "The porch can be read as an exemplar of a method by which a small physical change—a layering-over of air adhered to an existing fabric—can bring about a delicate tuning of persons with place."[20] How a porch embraces paradox makes that tuning possible—mixing inside with outside, public with private. Like masks, porches filter and connect; they are ready-made devices for the contradictions of social distancing, close enough for conversation but far enough for safety. Porches also embody resiliency and hold clues for adapting to change. Just as they shed rainwater, accept winds, and generally temper climate, porches also expose us to climate's crisis. Stepping out on a porch lays bare climate change and urges action, which is to say a porch is more than method—it is practice.

The pandemic has been a reminder that porches are more than passive attachments to supply fresh air, contented sleep, or relaxed conversation. Tuning person and place, they are spaces for radical practice. Unlike the patriarchal household, bell hooks identifies the porch as "a democratic meeting place, capable of containing folks from various walks of life, with diverse perspectives."[21] For her, this "free-floating space" is "a small everyday place of antiracist resistance" where she and her sisters and mother could "practice the etiquette of civility" in the face of racism.[22] Porches anchor practices amid social reckoning, environmental crisis, and the pandemic's many displacements of body and community. Remember the gratitude shown to healthcare workers from porches, balconies, and open windows? A porch enables ethical practice and active reflection; it is a tuning place of resilience and resistance. On the porch, we can take a hard look at systemic flaws in society and consider how that warmer breeze we feel on our skin blows across a changing planet.

Charlie Hailey is an architect, a professor at the University of Florida, and the author of **The Porch: Meditations on the Edge of Nature** *(2021).*

**The screened-in porch offers fundamental environmental-
and social-health benefits.** / Aidan Hailey

Postpandemic Transparency

Aki Ishida

Lacaton & Vassal's permeable architecture offers an antidote to hermetically sealed air-conditioned buildings.

—

Some spatial practices that emerged during the pandemic—including the use of partially covered outdoor spaces, such as patios, porches, and sidewalk dining sheds—have brought new life to building perimeters. These spaces can increase inhabitable spaces to live, work, and play and bring social cohesion and safety to a neighborhood. For example, the buildings by Anne Lacaton and Jean-Philippe Vassal are characterized by partially covered outdoor living spaces. Although not designed explicitly in response to public health needs, the structures enable relatively safe social gathering in naturally ventilated areas and suggest how we might create more permeable boundaries. Lacaton & Vassal's tactics include lessons from the transitory architecture of Niger, the adaptation of horticultural buildings for human inhabitation, and the use of transparent materials that are sustainable, adaptable, and affordable.

Vassal practiced urban planning in Niger early in his career and learned about transitory architecture that can be altered effortlessly according to climatic or privacy needs. He also observed that the site for a building extends beyond its envelope. On a dune looking down on the Niger River, he built his house out of straw, twigs, and rice mats. The house framed the view toward Niamey, the capital city, where, at night, the fires in the village in the distance served as his nighttime illumination. During the pandemic, such an expanded understanding of a site can heighten connections between people and their community while maintaining a social distance. Although protective barriers erected for social distancing can reinforce separations between people, some virus protection measures—including dining sheds placed outside restaurants—blur physical boundaries between inside and outside. Often built with a level of porosity or transparency, these structures can extend visual connections between people and places; they add more "eyes on the street," as Jane Jacobs writes in *The Death and Life of Great American Cities*, and create chance encounters that were previously absent.[23]

Upon their return from Niger to Bordeaux, France, Lacaton & Vassal continued to study botanical gardens and greenhouses that apply tempering strategies appropriate for the climate. Fascinated by the economy and pragmatism that enabled control of climatic conditions with high precision for delicate plants, they appropriated horticultural technologies for spaces of everyday human living, modulating water, temperature, and light. Unlike the tightly sealed glass curtain walls prevalent in contemporary workspaces and residential buildings, the ease of operability and adjustability offers a sense of agency for users. Lacaton & Vassal's winter garden walls and roofs are often lightweight plastic, requiring less steel and concrete structure and less specialized glazer labor. Subsequently, the partitions are significantly lower in material and labor costs and faster to install than glass. Furthermore, the doors and ventilators can be operated easily by hand because of their light weight.

The work of Lacaton & Vassal suggests ways toward economic, environmental,

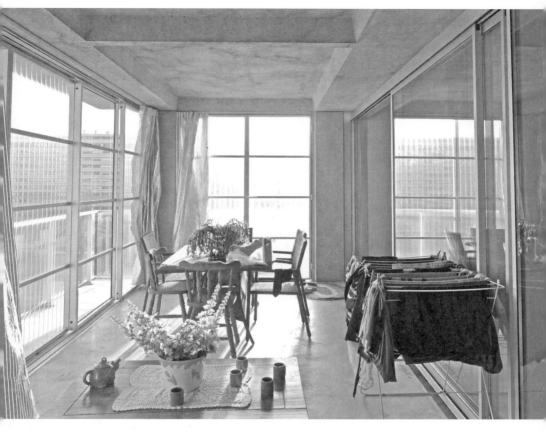

**Lacaton & Vassal, view of wintergarden extension at Cité du Grand Parc,
Bordeaux, France, 2016** / Philippe Ruault

and social sustainability. Lessons from the permeable boundaries of their architecture not only help to mitigate the virus and keep people safe during a pandemic but also offer—in their word—a "luxury" of expanded spaces and freedom of use for decades to come.

Aki Ishida is an associate professor of architecture and the interim associate director of School of Architecture + Design at Virginia Tech and the author of the book **Blurred Transparencies in Contemporary Glass Architecture (2020).**

Biochromic Window

Kyoung Hee Kim

Microalgae-infused building facade systems can improve indoor air quality, daylighting, and energy savings.

—

People spend the majority of their time indoors. During a worldwide pandemic, people have even less outdoor access. Potential advantages of interacting with nature have been well researched, including stress reduction, psychological restoration, and the promotion of physical activity, mental health, and social cohesion.[24] Conversely, there is a correlation between air pollution and adverse health effects. While CO2 is not often considered a pollutant, the gas can indicate low ventilation rates and the presence of harmful pollutants. The building sector plays a vital role in human health as well as energy savings and carbon reduction. These needs can be addressed with Biochromic Windows that incorporate multifunctional microalgae to improve occupant well-being, energy efficiency, and carbon neutrality.

The Biochromic Window design meets a variety of technical and programmatic performance data. For example, the geometry of the bioreactor responds to different climate zones and building orientations where solar irradiances vary. The latticelike structure of the system, which functions as a microalgae bioreactor, provides a balance between algae cultivation and the occupant's views and access to daylight. The interlocking composition allows multiple algae cultures to grow, so that the system offers biological redundancy if a monoculture fails. In addition, the network of modular units filled with microalgae may be adapted to different spatial and temporal scales. The modular construction thus allows for partial or full coverage of a building's surface area, and various configurations can be devised for different functional and aesthetic needs.

With various configurations composed of screens, louvers, and fins, the system regulates energy transfer between indoor and outdoor spaces by controlling solar glare, daylighting, views, microalgae growth, and aesthetics. With the ability to change the density and tint of microalgae, the Biochromic Window offers good shading efficacy and daylighting penetration, which also impacts energy savings. The heat energy stored in the system can be reclaimed for space heating and domestic hot water, resulting in additional energy savings. Room air circulation provides the system with dynamic insulation properties and reduces the heating and cooling loads.

CO2 and sunlight are essential for microalgae growth. The Biochromic Window utilizes room air with occupant-generated CO2—and, in return, produces oxygen-rich air tied to a centralized air-handling unit. The photosynthesis-based decarbonization capability also provides financial incentives—from carbon credits to high-value bioproducts—making microalgae-clad buildings more appealing to occupants, industry professionals, and stakeholders. In postpandemic architecture, the biological integration of microalgae in window assemblies can improve environmental performance, as well as human health and well-being, capitalizing on the symbiotic relationship between users and nature.

Kyoung Hee Kim is an associate professor in the School of Architecture at the University of North Carolina at Charlotte and the founder of EcoClosure.

**Detail of algae-infused Biochromic Window,
University of North Carolina at Charlotte** / Mike Basher

Fertilize, Don't Sterilize

Ted Krueger

The cultivation of beneficial environmental microbes is a fundamental step toward reducing pathogens in our environment.

—

The invocation of the War Powers Act in the fight against COVID-19 is a manifestation of our relationship to the microbial world. We routinely sanitize our hands and the surfaces we touch, and we develop antimicrobial coatings for materials in an effort to surround ourselves with microbial emptiness believing that then, we will be safe. When sick, we attempt to do the same with antibiotics—and have done so for decades—destroying the gut microbiome and assuming it rebuilds to a healthy state. But now we are beginning to realize that both our individual and collective microbiomes have been changing and a host of new diseases have resulted. Our efforts to keep the hands sanitized have culminated in our carrying a reservoir of drug-resistant bacteria with us. We feel ourselves in danger, so we wipe the surface clean of any inhabitants. These strategies express our fear and ignorance of this invisible world and often backfire. We don't yet have the knowledge or technology to target specific pathogens nor the ability to understand the rich and exotic ecosystems that we destroy.

Part of the problem of our relationship to the microbiota is that we identify ourselves as separate from them. Recent studies indicate that microbes make up a significant fraction of our bodies and undertake much of the work. A functional analysis of what we consider to be human will show much is microbial instead. With respect to diseases, we find that the microbiome plays a vital role in immune function both inside our body as well as on its surface. Our microbiome is in a constant state of transition and is in a reciprocal relationship with the microbiomes of the built and natural environments we inhabit.

Well-developed microbial ecosystems use all available resources, leaving it difficult for interlopers to gain a foothold. Rather than vacant, sterile surfaces, perhaps we should favor instead enriched microbial communities inoculated, strengthened, and maintained through architectural probiotics. Unfortunately, we are locked into a predator-prey evolutionary cycle with viruses, and it's not going our way. We may benefit instead from partnerships at the microbial scale, allies that can rapidly respond through population dynamics and mutations that can match those of the pathogens.

It is clear that we can contract diseases from the environment. Is it possible that we could acquire immunity from it as well?

Ted Krueger is an associate professor at the Rensselaer School of Architecture.

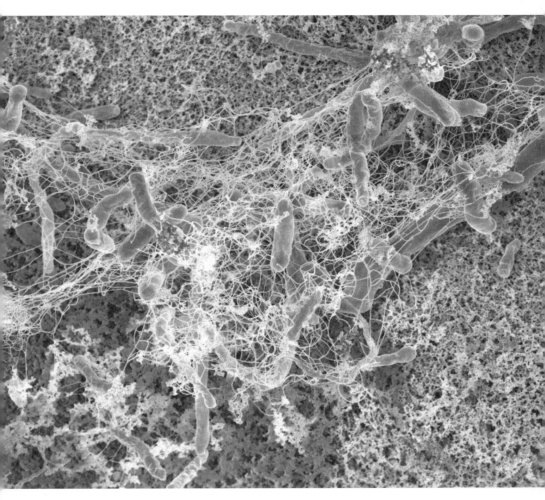

Graeme Bowles and Steven Lower, electron micrograph of bacteria biofilm, National Science Foundation, 2011 / Graeme Bowles and Steven Lower, National Science Foundation

Salutogenic Design

Angela Mazzi

Healthcare environments should focus on healing and not disease.

—

Salutogenesis is a concept of particular relevance in a pandemic. Coined by medical sociologist Aaron Antonovsky in 1979, the term is derived from the Latin *salus* (health) and Greek *genesis* (origin) and refers to the source of people's ability to maintain good health under stress.[25] Salutogenesis is rooted in the resources we have to cope. I use the analogy of a video game in which coins boost your health while hazards drain it. In a state of homeostasis, you have the resources to cope. However, if circumstances deplete your resources faster than you can acquire new ones, you enter a state of homeostenosis, a condition of frailty in which one little thing can throw off your balance.

When people contract the coronavirus disease, healthy people generally don't get very sick, but frail people tend to get very ill because they don't have the physical resources to cope. There's still so much we don't understand about COVID-19 regarding its long-term effects, adaptation speed, risk factors, and so on. This uncertainty itself causes stress, resulting in greater homeostenosis for everybody. While we can't control the stress, we can give you more coins (resources) to help you manage it. A fundamental question in our work is this: How can the environment restore you so that you have a better ability to cope and feel better?

There are five aspects we consider for salutogenic design. Self-efficacy refers to the tools to manage a situation. Relaxation response provides restorative benefits. Biophilia incorporates meaningful connections to nature. Prospect and refuge deliver a sense of protection and psychological safety. Finally, a sense of coherence facilitates understanding. Coherence, in particular, has been significantly diminished during the pandemic, with worker shortages, employees not returning to the office, and individuals now questioning what they were doing before COVID-19. People are seeking meaning and quality of life more than ever, and their environment should be supportive, manageable, and comprehensible.

TriHealth's Harold M. and Eugenia S. Thomas Center (completed in 2020) is integrated with these five principles of salutogenesis.[26] Although designed before the emergence of COVID-19, the entire building was planned around salutogenic principles that have benefited patients and healthcare workers during the pandemic. Connections to nature appear throughout the facility, with accessible outdoor areas at every level and landscaping integrated throughout the building—such as a garden adjacent to the infusion clinic. Spaces are inherently adaptable, providing enhanced flexibility. For example, during the pandemic, family and doctor meetings shifted from the consult rooms to the outdoor spaces to take advantage of fresh air and more opportunities for social distancing. The building's circulation enables one-way traffic flows, thus reducing chances for virus transmission. A luminous, generously sized central lobby eases visitor navigation and comprehension.

COVID-19 has brought significant changes to medicine. Healthcare is a very risk-averse field, and any change is met with skepticism. However, with the pandemic, maintaining the status quo suddenly became riskier than taking a different approach despite the inherent uncertainties. The medical field

GBBN, view of the lobby, TriHealth Harold M. and Eugenia S. Thomas Comprehensive
Care Center, Cincinnati, Ohio, 2020 / GBBN

discussed ideas like telehealth, changes
to waiting rooms, and biophilic strategies
for a long time, but changes didn't happen
until the alternatives became worse.
We now know that the status quo is no
longer an option—we have to invest in
more than minimum standards. We must
pursue the principles of salutogenesis in
the design of healing environments.

*Angela Mazzi is an architect, researcher,
and a principal at GBBN Architects.*

Air-Conditioning: The Social Machine

Liz McCormick

Human society's pursuit of comfort and hygiene has resulted in the self-defeating separation from nature.

———

We now exist in an era defined by human activity. Culturally, the Anthropocene is marked by the domination and commodification of nature—the rejection of which has shaped the foundation of modern mechanical engineering.[27] However, air-conditioning technologies have become a welcome luxury in many climates, though not without cultural, environmental, and economic implications. Adopting air-conditioning as the primary thermal strategy has supported global trends toward sealed, fully conditioned buildings, regardless of climate, health, culture, and local identity. Isolated from the natural rhythms of the outdoor environment, machines are used to produce static, neutral conditions that deliberately isolate the occupant from exterior conditions perceived to be undesirable and unhealthy. However, this phenomenon is not just technical—it is profoundly social and behavioral.

Culturally, climate control and social status are intimately connected as are conceptions of hygiene and cleanliness that have driven our relationship with the indoor environment.[28] In much of the literature, nature is portrayed as unclean and unsophisticated, where dirt can signify disorder, immoral ways of living, and even danger.[29] However, the human relationship with germs and cleanliness is actually a relatively new construct stemming from social perceptions of health and hygiene.[30]

For example, self-service grocery stores—made possible by innovations in refrigeration technologies—emerged rapidly in the United States in the early twentieth century. This shift was also supported by the development of cellophane, the disposable, transparent, and sanitary packaging film that not only revolutionized the way consumers purchased food but also how they perceived food quality.[31] Not only could consumers see the product that they were buying, but they could also determine that it was clean and untouched by human hands—playing upon germ phobias associated with human touch.[32] Social notions of health and hygiene throughout everyday aspects of modern life supported the popularity of transparency, which quickly became an icon of modernity.[33]

This notion developed concurrently with the invention of the curtain wall and the development of the all-glass archetype, which was largely influenced by the machine-made aesthetic that captivated early modernists. This system proliferated as the predominant building enclosure method in Europe and the United States and was identified as "the new vernacular" in 1957.[34] At this juncture in time, the facade became a thin, passive recipient of differential conditions between inside and out, and concerns of indoor air quality and human health were largely ignored.

Conceptions of human health have been influenced by cultural theories of hygiene and social demands to avoid germs. Unfortunately, this notion has driven humans further indoors and separate from the richness of the natural biome. By understanding that our relationship with conditioning machines has been determined as much socially as scientifically, we can begin to approach the problem without leaning on machines to solve it. Instead, designers must pursue a path to healthy buildings that embraces both technology and society concurrently.

Air-conditioning units in Mumbai, India / Blaine Brownell

*Liz McCormick is an assistant professor
in the School of Architecture at the
University of North Carolina at Charlotte.*

Breathing is Spatial

Michael Murphy

The pandemic reinforced the concept of breathing as a spatial act that is a fundamental right of all.

———

In the realm of rights, the right to breathe is of the highest order. Without breath, there is no life. But to breathe freely, as we have learned over the course of recent events, is not a guarantee. As an individual, breathing air free of the novel coronavirus requires spaces filled with exchanged or decontaminated air. Those spaces are not always in our control, or equally accessed, or designed with fresh, disease-free air as their primary concern.

This failure is a failure of our built world, one in which the pandemic reveals rights rescinded and hindered. These rights are facilitated by the structural injustices that lead to inequitable distribution of services (like housing or healthcare) and are managed, mitigated, and filtered through buildings. It is architecture, then, that is the limiting factor for the right to clean air because it is architecture that determines whether we have access to it or not.

Spatial rights have been largely understood as collective rights. Theorist Henri Lefebvre and later geographer David Harvey describe the right to the city as a common, collective right determined by common, collective action, "since transformation inevitably depends upon the exercise of a collective power to reshape the process of urbanization."[35]

But radical geographers remind us that the built world around us will always reinforce the power relationships of our social order. Space and justice are inextricably linked and in dialogue with ever-changing power dynamics. In this argument, the collective injustices of the spatial disciplines (racism, police violence, surveillance, segregation) are impossible to resolve. Designers and planners are left wondering where just planning solutions, as a set of actions, might be enacted without reinforcing oppressive power over relationships.

The pandemic offers us a solution to resolve this paralysis that has plagued the design disciplines for generations. We—nearly all eight billion people on the globe—are collectively awakening to our health and our access to each breath spatially. We are experiencing a spatial awakening: breathing is a spatial problem.

And while a range of design strategies—policies, standards, measurements, new structures—can be deployed to ensure that we breathe freely, there is an opportunity to propose that the contamination of air is not a simple issue managed only by changing the HEPA filter. It, instead, moves architecture into a new essentialism of fundamental rights hindered and provided. These are rights over which we can more clearly and succinctly demand control—namely, how our built world enables and inhibits access to that most fundamental human right we have: the right to breathe.

Michael Murphy is the founding principal and executive director of MASS Design Group.

**MASS Design Group, Gheskio Cholera Treatment Center,
Port au Prince, Haiti, 2015** / Iwan Baan

Chapter Three

INTERVENTIONS

Prevention and control methods to monitor, protect, and adapt postpandemic spaces

The Centers for Disease Control and Prevention (CDC) outlines a four-goal strategy to monitor, assess, and communicate information about the spread of infectious diseases.[1] The first goal, to "detect, promptly investigate, and monitor emerging pathogens," has relevance to the built environment.[2] Buildings are generally not equipped to monitor occupant health or detect illness. However, advances in sensor technology, artificial intelligence, and wireless power and communications are bringing monitoring capabilities to architecture.

"The quantified self," a term coined by *Wired* editors Gary Wolf and Kevin Kelly in 2009, describes the burgeoning trend of health tracking among individuals.[3] Information technology and facilities management experts Erik Jaspers and Eric Teicholz have adapted this concept to architecture with "the quantified building."[4] As wireless sensors proliferate in the built environment, they gather a growing volume of data about the behaviors of building components and their occupants. "Imagine having systems in place that could capture this data and use it in real time to adjust behavior and signal human intervention as needed," Jaspers and Teicholz write.[5] "Imagine being able to analyze the accumulation of this data over time to assess structural improvements and optimize operations." Such capabilities are advancing rapidly, and the quantified building will play a significant role in future disease mitigation.

In addition to detection, the CDC has established the Hierarchy of Controls for limiting the spread of disease.[6] The hierarchy diagram is an inverted pyramid with the least effective control (i.e., PPE) at the bottom and the most effective (i.e., hazard elimination) at the top. The level 3 category, engineering controls (hazard isolation), relates directly to the design of buildings and spaces. Engineering controls include changes to building envelopes and mechanical systems to increase the fresh-air exchange rate, topics addressed in the previous chapter.[7] These also include better filtration of recirculated air via upgraded HVAC system filters and portable air purifiers.

Physical barriers are another form of engineering control.[8] Partitioning spaces to control illness is similar to the concept of quarantine. Given that distance and transmission medium influence spread, dividing the air into isolated zones makes logical sense. The proliferation of plexiglass sneeze guards and space dividers during the COVID-19 pandemic embodies this idea. However, many factors—including airflow and human behavior—contribute to spreading a virus in space. As a result, studies have revealed that physical barriers are not foolproof solutions and may provide a false sense of security.[9]

The removal of pathogens has not been a traditional function of buildings. Sanitation efforts begun in the mid-nineteenth century have encouraged improved hygiene standards, and the use of cleaning products has since been a primary means of eradication. More recently, antimicrobial coatings have made it possible for surfaces to play a role in hazard elimination. In the early onset of the pandemic, scientists demonstrated that COVID-19 could be transferred not only between two people but also between a surface exposed to the virus and an individual coming into contact with it.[10] Although it was later demonstrated that the virus is more effectively transmitted via airborne droplets, virus viability remains a threat on some materials. The swiftly growing antimicrobial-coatings industry is now thought to be valued in the billion-dollar range.[11] Other emerging eradication strategies include electrified air filtration and far ultraviolet-C (far-UVC) lighting, both addressed in this section.

This chapter includes a variety of types of interventions, some of which have overlapping aims. Most contributions focus on the materials and methods used to address the environmental health challenges posed by the pandemic. Some of these interventions focus on detection, whereas others pertain to engineering controls and isolation. Yet another set of examples addresses new challenges that have intensified with the coronavirus disease. For example, acoustics is one area of significant concern today, given the prevalence of video teleconferencing in spaces not initially designed for such activities. Therefore, proposed acoustic modifications operate as interventions that address noise as an environmental quality concern.

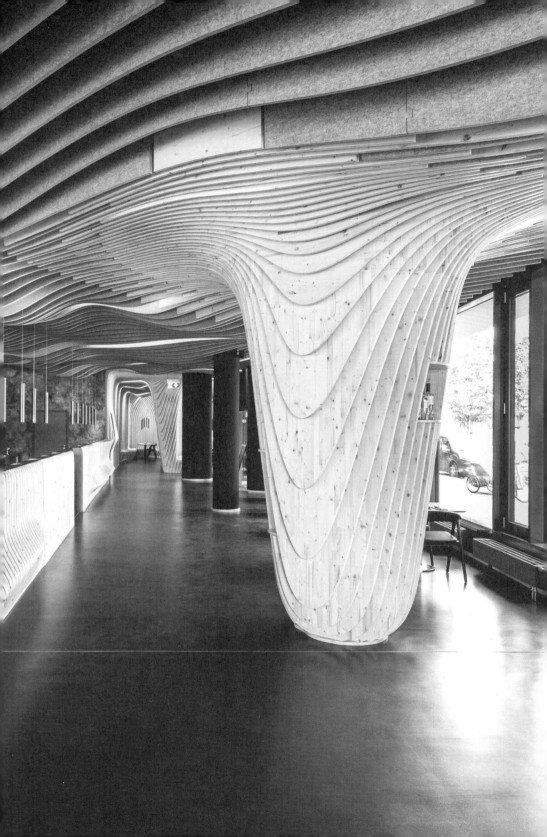

Occupant Health Monitoring

Mona Azarbayjani and Hamed Tabkhi

**Smart sensors mitigate the spread
of disease while protecting privacy.**

—

The increased growth of chronic illnesses
and epidemic viruses prompts the need
for innovative smart building technologies
that help prevent, mitigate, and control
the spread of highly contagious diseases.
In our current society, people spend more
than 90 percent of their time indoors, and
buildings play a significant role in human
health and the spread of illness.

Artificial intelligence (AI) and smart
technologies can revolutionize interior
environments by providing fully integrated real-time sensing, intelligent
processing, and extensive communication.
Emerging internet of things (IoT) devices
offer promising approaches for gathering valuable data and utilizing machine
learning to optimize occupant health.
Architects can ensure that these devices
are incorporated into a building's design
so that they function optimally during
the operation phase to monitor the user's
well-being.

New thermal infrared camera technologies offer an excellent means to collect
an occupant's temperature data as part of
a no-contact risk-management strategy.
Since the emergence of the COVID-19 pandemic, the noninvasive nature of thermal
cameras to monitor occupant body temperature has encouraged the adoption of
these devices to detect potentially infected
subjects. This health-monitoring platform
leverages simple visual red, green, and
blue (RGB) and thermal cameras to create
a multimodal sensing setup. In this intelligent system, the components are the
occupants, the built environment, and the
correspondence between the two. The

data streams produced by these three
components are captured continuously.

Building-integrated sensors allow
the collection of unlimited information
regarding occupant behavior and environmental properties, while real-time
analysis provides insightful feedback. This
camera-based evaluative system collects
several types of simultaneous data about
human physical and physiological measures in a control loop. The dual-camera
platform extracts the desired information
without identity checking, providing
a data-collection tool that is both secure
and efficient. This AI-powered approach
adds the power of deep learning to building-
based monitoring, providing reliable
intelligence about occupant biometrics
for public health oversight, including
pandemic control and prevention. This
knowledge will begin to fill significant gaps
in public health data without jeopardizing
occupant privacy. The continued integration of AI into the future workspace
will transform the smart environment
into an intelligent habitat.

*Mona Azarbayjani is an associate
professor and director of graduate
programs in the School of Architecture
at the University of North Carolina
at Charlotte.*

*Hamed Tabkhi is an associate professor
in the Department of Electrical and
Computer Engineering at the University
of North Carolina at Charlotte and
the founder and director of the
Transformative Computer Systems and
Architecture Research (TeCSAR) lab.*

A simulated thermal camera rendering of an office environment (top) and a simulation of artificial-intelligence-powered occupant monitoring in an office environment (bottom) / Mona Azarbayjani

Black Flower Antenna

Felecia Davis

A powerful electromagnetic receiver highlights the socioeconomic disparities present within the invisible urbanism of the internet.

———

The arrival of the COVID-19 virus eased the way for people to indirectly experience the invisible ocean of electromagnetic waves that can both connect people as well as atomize and separate us each into a distinct "I." *Black Flower Antenna*, a project exhibited at the Museum of Modern Art in spring 2021 as part of Reconstruction: Architecture and Blackness in America, uses the invisible media of electromagnetic waves making up Wi-Fi, radio, and Bluetooth technologies present everywhere to draw attention to an invisible urbanism that enmeshes our cities and spaces. The sound emitted by the antenna makes it possible for people to perceive invisible electromagnetic waves that would otherwise be imperceptible.

The *Black Flower Antenna* installation is a symbolic responsive structure and receiving antenna. It comprises thirty-four industrially knitted cones embedded with pink copper yarns that transmit electromagnetic waves via high-pitched live sounds in the gallery. The antenna can be tuned to pick up the sound of Wi-Fi, Bluetooth, or other currents flowing through a room. The *Black Flower Antenna*, composed of electromagnetic waves, makes visible the workings of an invisible urbanism that floats above the physical city.

These invisible waves represent a new global ocean of communication that allows people to exchange experiences, witness, give and receive care, and do thousands of other activities via the internet. Yet traversing this ocean in our everyday practices is as perilous as crossing the Atlantic during the Middle Passage. People start as humans and end up as property—data points in a database used for many different ends. By making this imperceptible information perceptible, The Black Flower Antenna reminds us of this other space of invisible information that is also characterized by unjust systems, such as redlining, exclusion, and extraction of service and profit from unknowing and unwilling bodies. This reality is especially pervasive in the United States, which has very few policies concerning these activities.

Materials to make the antenna can also be used to make antennas in clothing that can send signals from a body for others to monitor. Telehealth forces architects, designers, physicians, and others concerned about giving people care and wellness to consider spaces where we care for people, such as the hospital. If a person can wear something on their body that informs a nurse or doctor digitally through a computer about their condition, is it possible that they are able to avoid traditional medical facilities?

Felecia Davis is an associate professor in the College of Arts and Architecture at Penn State and a principal of Felecia Davis Studio.

Felecia Davis, *Black Flower Antenna*, Museum of Modern Art, New York, 2020 / Felecia Davis

Quiet Zone
Sven Erni and Jeffrey Ibañez

A space's acoustics are as crucial as good-quality air, light, and hygiene.

—

Acoustic design is more critical than ever. Acoustical characteristics are increasingly perceived as part of occupant well-being, which has become more important during the pandemic. Like clean air, proper lighting, or good hygiene, proper acoustics and the control of unwanted noise will play a crucial role in bringing people back to public buildings from their safe zones at home.

The pandemic has also led to a rethinking of how spaces are planned. Building occupants are more aware of how their surroundings affect one's sense of well-being and a feeling of security. Good acoustics can give occupants a feeling of calm to focus on a task with minimum disruptions. A product category we have been able to develop is the area of acoustic lighting. The combination of good light and acoustics offers excellent potential for improving occupant well-being. Flexibility is also crucial. Acoustic solutions should play a central role in defining zones, muffling conversations, and creating a sense of space.

Material-wise, we see the interplay of different materials, like concrete, wood, and recycled PET (polyethylene terephthalate), felt more often, not only as part of the furnishings but also in direct integration with architectural surfaces. We rely heavily on parametric design in our product development. Thanks to algorithms, we can model complex ceiling structures in very little time and program bespoke ceiling panels from them. We also see an ever-increasing need for color. The dreariness of pandemic life and the isolation at home have created a need for people to surround themselves with brightness and color.

One of our most pandemic-responsive products is Chatpod, a sustainable office pod solution. Before COVID-19, there was high demand for open telephone booths. However, today, people seek dedicated work environments, either for small groups or individual work. This desire to isolate is motivated by the proliferation of Zoom calls, during which people tend to talk louder than in a direct conversation. Chatpod is, therefore, an appropriate addition to open-office environments.

In postpandemic design, acoustics will be a standard requirement for spaces in all industries. The trend toward bespoke acoustic solutions is met with specific acoustic requirements on an individual level. Just as we have become accustomed to hygiene measures, in the future we will expect all buildings—including offices, restaurants, and public spaces—to have good acoustics.

Sven Erni is the manager and the cofounder of Impact Acoustic.

Jeffrey Ibañez is a designer and the cofounder of Impact Acoustic.

top: **Impact Acoustic noise-dampening interior, Fuji Yama, Nuremberg,
Germany, 2020** / Simeon Johnke bottom: **Impact Acoustic sound-absorbing panels
installed at Toradex AG, Horw, Switzerland** / Severin Ettlin

Wastewater Monitoring
Cynthia Gibas and Mariya Munir

Sampling wastewater is an effective method for limiting the spread of illness and can inform building design.

———

In the summer of 2020, as the pandemic was in full swing, we became aware of research indicating that SARS-CoV-2 was detectable in wastewater. Each appearance occurred in a given location before positive cases would arise. Our university task force was rapidly developing plans for a safe return to campus, and we sent a late-night proposal to the provost suggesting that we monitor building wastewater. The new chancellor arrived and agreed to fund a pilot study to cover all the dormitories. The state legislature was then informed of the effort, and suddenly, our pilot became a five-million-dollar project. Now we have a large lab, and we collect from thirty-seven different active sites.

Wastewater testing is a tough job. Some buildings are more conducive for sampling than others. The most important role is that of the person who sets up the autosamplers and collects them the following day, six days a week. It is physically demanding and exhausting work, and people get burned out. One must open up each autosampler, bring a gallon jug back to the lab, break down samples, and prepare them for molecular detection. Clogged sites are a frequent problem—you would not believe what people try to flush down a toilet. The flow rate varies greatly as well. Some sites have a very high flow rate, and sampling probes disappear because they get ripped off the hose by the high pressure. Other sites—such as sample isolation and quarantine buildings with very few occupants—have flow rates that are too low for sampling. Collection is everything, and we are always tinkering and optimizing.

Even after two years of constant adaptation, we continue to learn new techniques.

After the first semester, we published a case-study paper on our findings.[12] In dormitories without any sampling, COVID-19 clusters would grow to eight to ten people in size before contact tracing would trigger building-wide testing. However, in the buildings we sampled, clusters would only reach an average of two people before testing. We have been able to limit the spread of the virus more effectively because we can detect the early warning signs in the wastewater. The program has been very cost-effective for the university, which can avoid the typical approach of testing all campus personnel twice a week.

Our work involves virus surveillance sequencing, and we have compiled significant data sets. We know all the viral genomic sequences for tested individuals on campus and can tie the information back to each place of origin. By looking at samples in our wastewater archive, we can infer if we are missing cases in testing. We have learned that some buildings are more prone to becoming virus hot spots than others. We have data to support the claim that there are building-based transmission effects. For example, there have been more COVID-19 cases in dormitories with shared restrooms organized within a central core as opposed to facilities with distributed suite-based arrangements. We have also detected geospatial effects of transmission. We have tracked more significant clustering effects from buildings organized around shared quadrangle spaces. Although the dormitories are separate structures, they behave as if they are connected from a pandemic perspective.

In the future, our findings have the potential to inform the way buildings and

Cynthia Gibas and Mariya Munir test wastewater for COVID-19 at the University of North Carolina at Charlotte, 2021 / Kat Lawrence

spaces are organized to limit the spread of disease. We currently work with researchers who employ building-information modeling and geographic-information systems to map hot spots and simulate transmission as a spatio-temporal phenomenon. We are also seeing laboratory-testing capabilities become more distributed. A goal would be for each location to test and report its own samples rather than move material between sampling sites and a traditional lab. However, this capability is still developing and can lead to false positives—similar to antigen- versus PCR-based testing in individuals. Regardless of the techniques employed, wastewater testing is rapidly gaining traction as a way to control the spread of infectious diseases. We have been approached to include prisons, schools, and other facilities in our ongoing analysis, and the interest in this work continues to grow. Wastewater monitoring is now a national priority.

Cynthia Gibas is a professor of bioinformatics at the University of North Carolina at Charlotte and the founder of the North Carolina Urban Microbiome Project.

Mariya Munir is an assistant professor of civil and environmental engineering at the University of North Carolina at Charlotte.

EcoAcustica

Andrea Giglio, Maia Zheliazkova, and Ingrid Paoletti

The pandemic has inspired new thinking about acoustics in cities and household environments.

—

The COVID-19 pandemic has opened one of the most severe periods of social, economic, and environmental crisis since the World Wars. Moreover, the pandemic helped bring the relationship between human activities and noise pollution into the spotlight with the help of the mass media.[13] The consistent limitations to working activities and, in most cases, the complete closures of workplaces and the consequential reduction of commuting have led to, on the one side, a consistent decrease in urban noise levels and, on the other, an increase in household noise levels.[14]

During the initial lockdown, the reduction of noise from vehicles, aircraft, production plants, and people made urban public spaces so quiet that wild animals were motivated to explore central areas in cities.[15] At the same time, our homes were rendered entirely inappropriate for the multiple activities typically reserved for places such as offices and schools.[16]

To balance the needs of public health and economics, governments have been continuously enforcing various limitations, such as social-distancing regulations, following the trend curve of the epidemic spread.[17] This approach has led not only to restoring the soundscape to pre-Covid conditions but also to increasing sound sensitivity: noises not perceived as annoying before lockdowns now seem more disturbing.

Our lifestyles will have to continue to adapt to changeable restrictions because "future pandemics will emerge more often, spread more rapidly, and do more damage to the world economy."[18] From this perspective, acoustical research has become more imperative. Therefore, we must pursue bottom-up approaches to generate adaptable solutions capable of activating ecological responses amid the surrounding changes.

With the EcoAcustica research project, we have taken the first step toward a possible strategy for a postpandemic indoor acoustics design. We explore the design of high-performance acoustic surfaces based on the development of complex computational algorithms capable of generating customized solutions for interior spaces. In this work, we believe the approach to indoor acoustics should be oriented to three main goals: exploiting the scarcity of raw materials to develop sound sustainable materials, embedding human sound sensitivity in acoustic design through computational design, and integrating sensors and IoT technologies to provide activity-oriented sound solutions. We hope that effective research partnerships between academic institutions, corporations, and professional experts can deliver measurable results in acoustic applications in the built environment.

Andrea Giglio is an architect and PhD candidate in sound responsive systems in the Department of Architecture at the Politecnico di Milano.

Maia Zheliazkova is an architect and PhD candidate in the Department of Architecture at the Politecnico di Milano.

Ingrid Paoletti is an associate professor in the Department of Architecture and the founder of Material Balance Research Lab at the Politecnico di Milano.

Acoustic cork-wood panels developed within the EcoAcustica research project
with Wood-Skin srl and Tecnosugheri srl as industrial partners. The project was founded
by **Regione Lombardia.** / WoodSkin

Walls that Combat Disease

Bryan Glynson

Lime-based paint continuously fights the spread of illness without harming occupants.

———

The global health crisis triggered by the spread of deadly breakthrough infectious disease is making principal changes to our living environments and architectural designs at a magnitude our modern world has never seen. Most innocuous interior spaces are suddenly linked with the highest occupational risk, health hazards, and even deaths. Microbial particles, such as larger droplets and tiny aerosols, are naturally discharged in the course of basic human existence by activities like breathing and speaking. While outdoor settings are linked with minimal risk exposure for contracting an infectious disease, all indoor spaces are on the opposite side of the risk.

Walls represent the second largest disease transmitter after direct human-to-human touch. Instead of treating walls as a significant liability in spreading infectious illness, walls can be used to prevent disease. Antimicrobial paint has played a critical role in controlling infectious diseases since its inception more than a decade ago. The biotechnology company Alistagen Corporation first introduced this noninvasive functional coating. The efficacy of this nontoxic paint is perceived to become the standard protocol for all interior settings.

After introducing the first antimicrobial paint to the market, coating industries have recognized the importance of such treatment and have generated robust and consistent double-digit growth for the past ten years. What has become apparent is that this approach represents a delicate balance between safety and efficacy.

Achieving meaningful antimicrobial, biocidal, and biostatic effectiveness requires a delicate balance of technical prudence and cutting-edge bioengineering. Several corporations have attempted to devise treatments based on synthetically engineered biocides employing triclosan, quaternary ammonium chloride, silver, or copper, but these approaches have led to adverse human health effects and antimicrobial resistance. In contrast to these "overkill" treatments, the industrial antimicrobial coating Caliwel Bi-Neutralizing Agent (BNA) employs the natural mineral calcium hydroxide, or lime, which has been utilized in interior settings throughout human history. The self-propagated protocol of Caliwel BNA enables long-term efficacy without the risk and exposure to harmful elements caused by synthetically engineered biocides or the slow release of silver ions or copper particles in the environment. Upon exposure to this coating, viruses, bacteria, and fungi completely disintegrate with essentially no trace left. The treated surface size matters: the more treated surfaces, the higher level of protection.

Antimicrobial paint will be imperative in every architectural design from now on. With the arrival of the global pandemic, we cannot dismiss the role that omnipresent architectural surfaces play in our living and working settings. What makes the antimicrobial paint protocol necessary and effective is that it is noninvasive. The coating continuously combats the underlying causes of disease, staying one step ahead of microbial infection. If most architectural interior surfaces were treated with responsible antimicrobial coatings, the spread of pandemics would be significantly reduced.

Joanna Kosinska, *Untitled,* **2017** / Joanna Kosinska

Bryan Glynson is the chief executive
officer of Alistagen Corporation.

One Foot Forward

Nancy Mourad

Adding foot pulls to conventional doors is an effective, inexpensive, and widely applicable way to reduce touch-based transmission of infectious diseases.

—

If the purpose of design is to improve people's personal and societal well-being and happiness—and if doors constitute objects with which our bodies interact daily, in and out—then designing health-conscious doors must be an essential part of our design thinking for the future. While a door structure is important ergonomically for musculoskeletal health (a noncommunicable disease factor), the COVID-19 pandemic has proven that doors also play an essential role in contributing to—or curbing—the spread of communicable diseases. In addition, people's awareness of the function of doors in pathogen transmission increases their emotional toll due to the necessity of sanitizing or washing hands after contact.

Data has shown that germs can linger on an inanimate object, such as a doorknob, from seconds to days and can become the source of infection when touched and transferred to the mouth or respiratory system. The risk of transmission is elevated when such a surface is touched frequently. While touchless, hands-free, motion/infrared sensor door solutions have become an effective way to bypass this issue, these doors are not always practical for all door types and situations (e.g., restroom doors in a traditional restaurant). In addition, motion-sensor doors are often challenging to design and install, as they require a partial or complete reconstruction of the doorway. Such cost and set-up factors can hinder widespread implementation.

An alternative solution is to replace door handles with foot pulls. The simplicity of adding a foot-operated mechanism to practically any door—without the need to otherwise modify the door or frame—represents a viable, affordable, and widely replicable approach. This strategy not only contributes to reducing COVID-19 transmission but also diminishes the spread of future pandemics. Adding a foot pull requires little disruption to the door, and existing handles can be left in place. Foot pulls work best in retail, restrooms, and other public spaces that use conventional doors with little automation capacity or potential. When privacy is required, such as in single-stall toilets, the ideal mechanism also enables locking the door with the foot handle itself.

Now let's reimagine the whole experience of exiting a shop in New York or Istanbul—big cities with millions of touches per day on each door. And think of the impact of such a seamless experience on human well-being, requiring neither sanitization nor jeopardizing health through the avoidable spread of germs. This reality is achievable thanks to the design of a foot-operated door.

Nancy Mourad is a public health administrator and the managing director of Gulf Region for LifeSpeak.

A door foot pull installed in a public restroom, Charlotte, North Carolina / Blaine Brownell

CounterAct

Brent Peckover

**Far-UVC lamp technology can
significantly reduce pathogens
in occupied spaces.**

⸻

A 254-nanometer-wavelength light is
often used for UV disinfection, as it was
close to the optimum effectiveness
and easily produced by a mercury lamp.
However, the downside of 254-nano-
meter light is that it penetrates human
skin and eye tissue. The light negatively
affects these living cells, eventually resulting in cataracts and cancer. As a result,
254-nanometer light can only be used
when rooms are unoccupied. The problem
is that most viruses and bacteria travel
into spaces by hitching a ride on people
and animals. Therefore, once a sick person
enters a clean room, the area is no longer
pathogen-free.

Far-UVC technology represents
a technological breakthrough. Far UVC's
222-nanometer light effectively inacti-
vates pathogens but does not penetrate
larger objects in the same way. In humans,
far-UVC energy is absorbed mainly by
the dead-skin layer and the tear layer in
the eye, which means the light doesn't
have the same negative impact on living
cells since very little energy reaches them.
This high effectiveness against pathogens
with few adverse effects against human
exposure opens the possibility to use
far-UVC light in occupied spaces.

Christie CounterAct products with
Care222 technology are designed to
neutralize pathogens with people present. Care222 is also the world's first UVC
technology with a proprietary optical
filter that blocks potentially harmful UVC
wavelengths from being emitted. The light
can be used while a space is occupied,
disinfecting the area continuously while

being used. Now, when the next individual
enters the room, any pathogens from
the first person have the potential to be
inactivated.

People often ask, "How long does it
take for CounterAct to start inactivating
pathogens in a space?" The answer is
that it starts as soon as the Care222 lamp
is turned on. The fixture fully complies
with industry standards for human safety,
such as Conformite Europeenne (CE)
and Underwriters Laboratories (UL).
A September 2020 study by researchers at
Hiroshima University found that far-UVC
222 nanometer light effectively reduced
more than 99.7 percent of surface contamination of SARS-CoV-2, the virus that
causes COVID-19. When mounted 22 feet
above the floor, the CounterAct fixture covers approximately 350 square feet
of surface at tabletop height. The standard
fixture currently generates only far-
UVC light; however, the Krypton Chloride
Care222 lamp also generates a small
amount of purple-hue visible light, thus
indicating its functionality to users.

We envision a future where far-UVC
units are installed in all occupied spaces
and used to disinfect the air and surfaces
within building interiors actively. When
the next pandemic occurs, the potential to
measure a significantly reduced viral load
in occupied spaces due to far-UVC light
will be a worthwhile achievement.

*Brent Peckover is an engineer and
director of industrial applications
at Christie Digital Systems, USA, Inc.*

Christie, far-UVC-powered CounterAct lighting fixture / Christie Digital Systems

Urban Sun

Daan Roosegaarde

Far-UVC light can create virus-free, pedestrian-safe zones in public spaces.
—
The swift spread of the COVID-19 pandemic made many people reluctant to inhabit public spaces. However, the inoculating capabilities of far-UVC light have become more widely known as an antidote to aerosol-based pathogens. Although ultraviolet light has been used for years to eradicate unwanted microbes, traditional ultraviolet (UV) light of a 254-nanometer wavelength is not used in inhabited places because long-term exposure to this light is hazardous to the skin and eyes. However, far-UVC light with a wavelength of 222 nanometers is effective against pathogens and safe for people and animals.

The Urban Sun is a light fixture designed to illuminate and disinfect public spaces. Emitting far-UVC light in the 222-nanometer range, the fixture eradicates the coronavirus disease and other pathogens that fall within its radius of illumination. The Urban Sun is a single suspended source of light that projects a bright, forty-nine-foot (fifteen-meter) diameter disc on the ground that represents a pedestrian safety zone. The light was created by a team of designers and scientists from the Netherlands, the United States, Italy, Spain, and Japan based on recent scientific advances. The research that informed Urban Sun demonstrates that a 222-nanometer light quickly eradicates up to 99.7 percent of SARS-CoV-2, influenza, and other viruses. Based on the fixture's potential impact, we are developing another version with a much larger 37,670-square foot (3,500-square-meter) area of light.

In a world now filled with plastic barriers and social-distancing reminder signs, public spaces have become less inviting. At the same time, people now spend more of their time communicating digitally than in person than ever before. The Urban Sun offers a solution to our isolated existence, functioning as a welcoming light that invites people to resume safer face-to-face interaction in public spaces once more.

Daan Roosegaarde is a designer and the founder of Studio Roosegaarde.

Studio Roosegaarde, Urban Sun, Amsterdam, the Netherlands, 2019–2021 / Daan Roosegaarde

Enjoy the Silence

Asami Takahashi and Jason Lim

The design of a sophisticated sound-absorbing spatial installation shows promise for quieting noisy environments.

—

Enjoy the Silence was our entry for a 2019 exhibition called Unnatural Phenomena. We wanted to create an abnormal pocket of silence within an otherwise noisy and crowded exhibition space in response to this theme. The outcome was a sculptural installation—later named *Köral*—that emerged from our investigations into geometry, acoustics, and materiality.[20]

Curved, undulating forms based on hyperbolic geometry are abundant in nature—corals and lettuce, for example—and characterized by having maximal surface area. Similarly, our sculpture approximates the hyperbolic plane to create a large surface that absorbs sound. We wrote custom algorithms to generate these forms and evaluate their acoustic performance.

Our sculpture has a skeletal structure filled with substrate material with a high-absorption coefficient and is skinned by soft, colorful fabric. We considered *Köral* to be a prototypical acoustic system for the interior environment. It helps to reduce ambient noise levels and appeals to the visual and tactile senses. It can be placed as the backdrop for a Zoom call and used to partition off quiet study areas or more personal meeting spaces.

The importance of acoustics has often been underappreciated. Yet it is amplified today due to the pandemic, which has upended the way we work and live. Remote working and learning have become common, if not the norm. The home has merged with the office and school, which are conventionally designed to meet different spatial and performance requirements. The usual result is a cacophonous acoustic environment disruptive for both work and learning. Ongoing Zoom calls, family conversations, audio from disparate sources all contribute to a discordant sound field that distracts and renders speech less intelligible. Working parents and remote-learning children may struggle to complete their tasks as a result. Unfortunately, this exacts a toll on mental health and could adversely affect children's education in the long term.

Clearly, the pandemic has highlighted the importance of acoustic privacy and noise control. Even if the world transitions to a new normal that resembles prepandemic times, people will demand a higher standard of acoustic quality from their environments. We should rise to the challenge and address the aural dimension from the outset of any project and aim to design spaces that provide a gradient of acoustic environments that support different uses and are even enjoyable.

Asami Takahashi is the principal architect and cofounder of Yume Architects.

Jason Lim is the principal designer and cofounder of Yume Architects.

Yume Architects, *Enjoy the Silence*, in the exhibition Unnatural Phenomena, Singapore, 2019 / Yume Architects

The Coming Sensor Age

John Waszak

Building sensors will play essential roles in mitigating the spread of disease and reducing energy consumption.

———

Early in the pandemic, it became evident that low-occupancy buildings are just as expensive to run as fully occupied buildings. While many buildings had transitioned to lower-cost LED lighting and smart sensors to control lighting, the HVAC system, by and large, had to continue to operate at full-occupancy energy levels. With the complete return to the office uncertain for the foreseeable future, there is an opportunity for building-sensor technology to both enable that return and help buildings manage a range of occupancy levels. From this point forward, building sensors will play significant roles in two primary areas: pathogen risk mitigation and occupant-centric key performance indicators (KPIs).

Pathogen risk mitigation will involve monitoring everything in the prepandemic sensor toolbox—volatile organic compounds (VOC), CO2, particulates, air pressure, relative humidity—but with much more extensive distribution throughout buildings. It is not enough to know the airflow and exchanges through the primary HVAC return; one now needs to understand the number of air exchanges through each space. Pathogen risk mitigation has also brought UVC lighting to the forefront of disinfection initiatives, creating a market for UVC sensing devices in labs around the world and an opportunity for sensor deployment anywhere UVC is used in building environments.

Occupant-centric KPIs will shift the emphasis from buildings to occupants. For example, we will move away from tracking how much energy is required to run a building (i.e., kWh/m^2-yr) to how much energy is needed to run a building on an occupancy basis (i.e., kWh/occupant-yr). This shift has created a need for sensors to detect occupancy and optimize occupancy loads. HVAC, in particular, will need to move in the direction of motion-controlled lighting. Due to the longer time constants involved in heating and cooling, sensors and analytics will need to sense and predict occupancy such that smart HVAC environments can be set in motion ahead of likely occupancy. These interconnected HVAC environments will also need more sensors to manage spaces more effectively. Passive heating and cooling techniques will also come into play, integrating additional sensors and intelligence to feed into smart HVAC management. For instance, sunlight sensors and weather forecasts can feed into heating and cooling logic, reducing unnecessary set-point overshoot and undershoot. A related synergistic occupant-centric effect will be the demand for more comfortable workplaces to encourage employees to frequent the office, which will, in turn, improve occupant-based KPIs.

John Waszak is a computer engineer and the cofounder of L and M Instruments.

The increased interest in building sensors is evident in DIY devices, such as
Wilderness Labs' Meadow F7 Micro sensor / Jorge Ramirez

Catch-and-Kill Air Filtration

Luo Yu and Zhifeng Ren

Electrified folded-nickel foam eliminates virus transmission through mechanical systems.

—

SARS-CoV-2, which has been demonstrated to be easily transmitted through aerosols in the air, caused the pandemic. The virus brings a high chance of infection from aerosol transmission in any closed space through central air-conditioning systems.[21] The good news is that any biological species, including SARS-CoV-2, is not resistant to high temperatures.[22] Therefore, if an air-conditioning filter can be heated to a high temperature of up to 200°C, any coronavirus in the cycling air can be efficiently killed within a very short period of time.

Unfortunately, conventional filters made of fiberglass or aluminum mesh are difficult to heat or have large pores that cannot effectively catch and kill the virus in aerosols. However, commercial metallic mesh such as nickel (Ni) foam is electrically conductive, mechanically strong, and highly flexible. More importantly, it has a 3D network structure with many nonstraight channels and is highly porous with good air permeability. Therefore, the foam is a promising filter material for catching and killing the coronavirus in air-conditioning systems, especially when the material is pleated together with high-temperature filtering paper. However, because of the very low resistivity of Ni foam, it is extremely challenging to fabricate a Ni foam filter to achieve a sufficiently high temperature up to 200°C, and simply using one piece of Ni foam as a filter that meets the size requirement for HVAC systems and the US residential voltage requirement (110 volts) is not possible.

Considering the excellent flexibility of Ni foam, our strategy was to design a folded structure with a much larger resistance, together with high-temperature filter paper. After detailed calculations based on the HVAC and voltage requirements and numerous tests to evaluate the required time to reach a specific temperature, we fabricated a filter using six pieces of folded Ni foam connected electrically in a series for lab testing. This Ni foam–based filter device exhibited the ability to catch and kill aerosolized coronavirus particles and anthrax spores (a more infectious agent) when the Ni foam was heated to 200°C.

A new company, Integrated Viral Protection, was established to market mobile units and HVAC filters, eliminating any viruses and particles larger than 0.3 micrometers at an efficiency above 99.97 percent. The deployment of these novel mobile and HVAC units has had a dramatic impact on the COVID-19 pandemic and has been shown to reduce the risk of other airborne respiratory system viruses, both known and unknown.

Luo Yu is a postdoctoral researcher in the Department of Physics at the University of Houston.

Zhifeng Ren is the MD Anderson Chair Professor in the Department of Physics at the University of Houston.

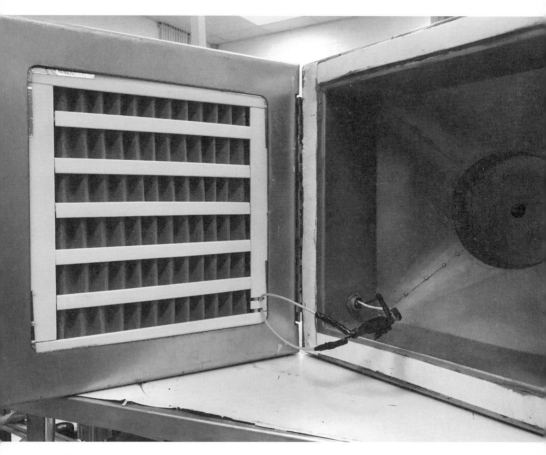

Filter made with folded nickel foam, University of Houston, Texas / University of Houston

Pandemic War Theater
Catty Dan Zhang

A time and motion study of COVID-19 safety measures in meat processing reveals new insights about worker exposure to the virus.

—

The Meat and Poultry Processing Workers and Employers Interim Guidance from the CDC and the Occupational Safety and Health Administration (OSHA), initially issued on April 26, 2020, amid the pandemic, outlines several categories of new safety protocols and procedures.[23] Particularly related to processing lines, the guidance illustrates four main tactics: maintain a certain distance between workers, alter the alignment of workstations, install physical barriers at locations, and control the origin and the direction of airflow generated by fans in the workspace. The suggested reconfigurations of facility layouts appear to be effective; however, no detail about the physical barriers, other than a few potential impermeable materials, is specified in the document.[24] An interesting architectural phenomenon emerged shortly after its implementation. Arrays of rectangular surfaces with various colors, transparencies, proportions, and rigidities populated along the assembly lines in meat-processing plants. Some of the improvised space dividers were suspended from rails, while others were attached to moveable frames made from lightweight materials, such as PVC pipes.

The generic plexiglass dividers installed in retail stores, offices, and public spaces block airborne particle travel pathways in a wide range of scenarios. However, the temporary architectural elements in meat- and poultry-processing facilities are situated within distinct and dynamic contexts. Physical barriers respond to explicitly categorized and highly repetitive activities involving products moving at constant paces, machines executing programmed motion sequences, and workers performing limited sets of predictable operations.[25]

Lines and Shields is a forensic visualization project that imagines forms of invisible particles modulated by the determinacy of motion sets and the informality of temporary dividers in the meat-processing industry instigated by COVID-19. Motion performed by machines and humans is captured in image sequences and interacts with reference planes of "digital air." The resulting flows then collide onto various compositions of rigid surfaces. This approach visualizes movement in homage to engineer Frank B. Gilbreth's scientific methods of quantifying time and motion in the human work process in assembly lines.[26] However, unlike Gilbreth's work, the research does not intend to establish new mathematical models to reform post-Covid-era meat processing. Instead, the analysis exposes the hybrid realities of the internal organization of contemporary food systems that laborers occupy. Here, the dynamic interactions between particles and temporary shields become measured instruments, revealing labor's effects on architectural spaces. This otherwise imperceptible information enables us to reconsider forms and systems of a productivity-driven infrastructure that supports the wellness of inhabitants by adding medium and atmosphere to the equation in design processes.[27] Ultimately, this analysis is not just about architectural materials and the speed of robots but also the distribution of air pockets, aggregated vortexes, puffs of heat and smell, and air currents that accelerate the spread of diseases.

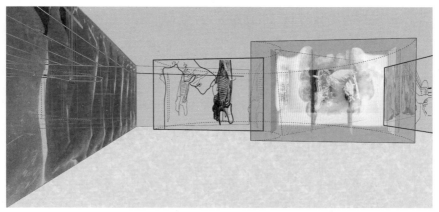

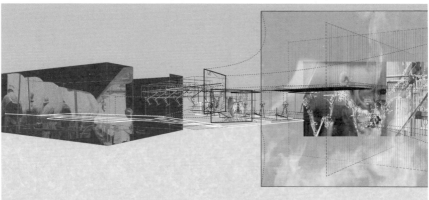

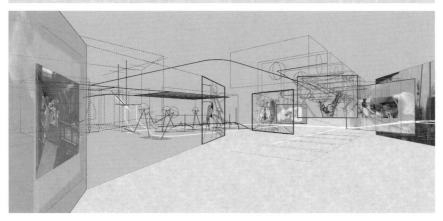

**Temporary Office, diagrams from the War Theater 2020s
visualization project, 2021** / Catty Dan Zhang

*Catty Dan Zhang is an assistant professor
at the University of North Carolina at
Charlotte School of Architecture and the
founder of Temporary Office.*

Chapter Four

NEW STRATEGIES

Updated approaches
to designing spaces
and systems for
pandemic-influenced
human activities

When the SARS-CoV-2 epidemic became a pandemic, human societies abruptly developed a fear of architecture. Buildings became magnifiers of contagion instead of shelters for protection. Informed by rapidly disseminated scientific studies, people grew afraid of the pathogen-harboring materials, germ-propagating mechanical systems, and populated spaces that could facilitate virus transmission. Limitations in the knowledge sharing between the fields of architecture and public health became immediately apparent. The fact that buildings were now designated viral superspreaders exposed the failures of the design and construction industry to prepare adequately for this kind of disease.

Over time, increased knowledge of the nature of virus transmission and the ability to limit its spread—albeit imperfectly and inconsistently—shifted the predominant mindset from fear to coping. The home was now the site of many additional activities, transformed into a surrogate workplace, school, gym, restaurant, and retail store. E-commerce soared as the online ordering of groceries and take-out delivery became more common. Medical and testing facilities became hot spots of activity. Office buildings, schools, and performance venues lay vacant. Airports became ghost towns as travel ground to a standstill.

As has often been said, life will not return to what it was before COVID-19. Talk of changing how we conduct activities began soon after the first stay-at-home orders went into effect. Shortly into the first lockdown measures, the world surprised itself with how quickly and effectively employees, teachers, and students pivoted their jobs and educations online—and how seamlessly brick-and-mortar shoppers shifted to online shopping. Even real estate went virtual, with 360-degree immersive walkthroughs. Speculations about the end of the office, the school, and the brick-and-mortar store proliferated in the wake of adequate digital substitutes.

Yet problems also surfaced. Socioeconomic disparities became more apparent as the wealthy vacated cities for vacation homes, leaving those less fortunate behind in more perilous conditions. Public transportation, a mobility lifeline for many carless individuals, suddenly seemed more hazardous. Hospitals became overcrowded—particularly with patients disproportionately representing underserved populations—

and set up makeshift clinics and testing centers in parking lots. Commercial and institutional buildings, although hardly occupied, continued to consume significant amounts of power due to their shortsighted, "always-on" systems design. Supply chains were disrupted, sending the price of lumber and other building materials to new highs. Long days of video tele-conferencing brought a new kind of fatigue, and many experienced increased levels of anxiety and depression from the isolation of remote life.

Such challenges have brought opportunities. In architecture, interior design, and urban planning, the optimal locations for various activities are being reconsidered. Home, work, and so-called third places—defined by sociologist Ray Oldenburg in reference to locations beyond home and work, such as cafes and pubs—are merging and expanding their programmatic territories.[1] Each location is now assimilating elements of the other two: households now accommodate more work, fitness, and entertainment activities than before the pandemic; workplaces are under pressure to incorporate more domestic comforts and ancillary activities to lure remote employees back to the office; and third places are expected to provide relaxing environments that can double as workplaces. In all such sites, the desire for improved air quality and access to green space is encouraging more open, biophilic designs. In addition, elevated awareness about the physical and sensory challenges many buildings pose for marginalized communities is leading to more inclusive design approaches.

Traditional programs are also being wholly reinvented. COVID-19 brought swift changes to medical facilities based on the necessity to address a global health crisis. Telehealth, mobile clinics, improved palliative care, and purposeful connections to natural environments are some of the transformations that will likely endure beyond the pandemic. Senior-living communities and low-income-housing typologies are being redesigned to protect vulnerable populations and encourage better mental and physical health. Retail is under pressure to accommodate significant changes in e-commerce and home delivery, curbside pickup, warehouse automation, and supply-chain optimization.

Pandemic transformations include design practice itself. Remote work has accelerated the use and advancement of digital tools to simulate immersive in-person experiences. Supply shortages and resource volatility are encouraging more adaptable, self-reliant, and environmentally responsible material strategies. There is an elevated recognition of the needs of marginalized communities for better inclusivity, mobility, and wayfinding. Interdisciplinarity is increasingly recognized as a necessity—not an option—as design teams seek to integrate a broader range of expertise. As a result, architects and designers are now in closer dialogue with ecologists, engineers, and public health experts to ensure better protections against future pandemics. Pandemic interdisciplinarity is exemplified by the emergence of architectural epidemiology, a new hybrid field created to address common environmental and social health-based knowledge gaps in the design process.[2]

As the myriad and diverse considerations presented in this chapter demonstrate, COVID-19 has precipitated massive changes in the ways we approach the functions and characteristics of the built environment. As a result, the ensuing years are likely to bring the most significant collective transformation to building design and construction since the postwar boom of the mid-twentieth century.

The Small House Model

Alexis Denton

There is an urgent need to redesign senior living communities to be smaller and more engaged.

———

Purpose-built senior living communities offer older adults the promise of a safe environment with social and cultural engagement opportunities. These environments house residents with vastly different needs along the continuum of care. For some, senior living is a choice; for others, a necessity. The quality of the environment varies greatly across the industry—the better communities function and feel like all-inclusive cruise ships; the worst, like warehouses. During the COVID-19 pandemic, the core promises of safety and engagement these environments provided were challenged by the fast transmission and severe outcomes in the older, often-frail population living within.

COVID-19 was felt most acutely in skilled nursing facilities (commonly referred to as nursing homes), where the most vulnerable residents live. In traditional skilled nursing, it's common to have shared resident rooms within interior neighborhoods that house forty to sixty people. These environments are typically sterile and institutional, resemble hospitals more than homes, and are overcrowded. A different model of skilled nursing facilities, the Small House model transforms an institutional environment to one that is residential and more in keeping with a typical, single-family home. In these Small House models, residents live in households of six to twelve people in private rooms with direct access to shared living, kitchen, and dining rooms. In addition, they operate with a small, dedicated team of caregivers—this is a crucial

element for reducing the transmission of infectious diseases. As a result, this model had significantly lower transmission and death rates than traditional skilled nursing facilities during the pandemic.

As a result of the Small House's success in keeping residents safe during the pandemic, other levels of care—notably memory care, assisted living, and even independent living—are transitioning to smaller scale, flexible-living environments. Instead of a cruise ship with large-scale centralized commons spaces that encourage many people to share the same area, the new model enables multiple hubs of smaller-scale decentralized commons that can change function as outside forces dictate. For example, a living room can transition into a small-scale dining room when it isn't safe to dine in large settings. Likewise, large-scale apartment buildings are broken down into smaller pods with their own entrances/exits. These function more like villages or pocket neighborhoods within a building. Additionally, outdoor spaces adjacent to each pod expand those common areas and serve as outdoor rooms that are purposefully designed to be enjoyed during every season.

In this approach, residents can isolate themselves safely with a small group of others during a pandemic or other disaster, lessening the risk of social isolation and its physiological effects. This approach creates a variety of social scales between private and public, functioning more like a city made up of distinct neighborhoods. There are more social spaces between the living unit and large-scale gathering spaces. Ultimately, the single "cruise ship" becomes a series of villages that make up a larger community.

Perkins Eastman, Goodwin House skilled nursing facility, Alexandria, Virginia, 2017 /
Sarah Mechling. Courtesy Perkins Eastman

The enduring design responses to COVID-19 aren't necessarily new to the industry; in many instances, the pandemic only exacerbated existing trends that are working to improve the quality of life of older adults. A resilient environment with increased flexibility, a greater variety of social scales, and more focus on transitional private-to-public space can help the industry honor its core promise of keeping residents safe and socially engaged.

Alexis Denton is an architect, a gerontologist, and an associate principal at Perkins Eastman.

Ecotone
Alper Derinboğaz

The postpandemic workplace should have a more direct connection with the outdoors.

——

While experiencing remote working interfaces during the pandemic, I further understood that workplaces are not only spaces for work but also spaces for gathering. Therefore, I believe the pandemic will dramatically change workplaces and the approach to creating these spaces. There is a misconception that working environments can only be indoors, and we now know that open spaces are safer for gatherings. I believe this idea will encourage architects to explore the potentials of transitional zones between inside and outside or between nature and buildings.

Ecotone is a postpandemic workplace that occupies a transitional space between education and industry. Located between two buildings, the project includes spaces for teaching, meeting, and flexible coworking. This hybrid space is part of a campus designed to spark innovation and develop new technologies.

The building aims to achieve a new fundamental relationship between roof and slab. Rethinking the conditions of theorist Marc-Antoine Laugier's Primitive Hut, a conceptual origin of architecture, the design consists of a simple column arrangement that is informed by the project's location in a high-wind and earthquake-risk zone. The slender columns—reminiscent of stalagmites or stalactites—expand at the ground and roof connections to support lateral loads in the self-supporting structure.

Developed during the global coronavirus pandemic, Ecotone proposes a new example for pandemic-resistant and sustainable office architecture, integrating outside areas, planting, and protected yet fluid office zones. Providing a more thoughtful office environment that prioritizes hygiene and safe places for individual and group working, Ecotone compartmentalizes the interior with transparent surfaces, allowing spaces to be safely divided but still feel open, light, and engaged with the outdoors.

Many of the same features that make spaces more resistant to pandemics also have ecological benefits and better indoor environmental qualities. The green spaces within, between, and around Ecotone break up the solid mass and bring in fresh air and offer connections to nature. These spaces contribute to a safer environment, creating zones for distancing, breezes that carry away bacteria, and increased oxygen from plants nearby.

Open-air zones in the plan layout provide informal meeting areas, avoiding closed group spaces. In addition to the outdoor rooms, plantings bring oxygen inside the building, and natural ventilation provides clear airflows throughout the interior spaces without relying on mechanical systems. The open and semi-open circulation spaces maximize the natural airstream between the inside and outside via air movement from low to high openings.

Disrupting the conventional office paradigm, Ecotone will foster the investigation and generation of new methods of creating workspaces between nature and architecture.

Alper Derinboğaz is an architect and the founder of Salon Alper Derinboğaz.

Salon Alper Derinboğaz, Ecotone, Yıldız Technical University, Istanbul, Turkey /
Salon Alper Derinboğaz

Supply Chain Resilience

Alexander Franco

In the future, we can avoid the kind of super disruption in building-material supply chains caused by COVID-19.

———

The coronavirus pandemic wreaked havoc on supply chains throughout the world. The affected areas included the forest-products industry and, especially, the lumber industry, with the price of lumber rising in the United States to levels not witnessed since the nation's housing boom of more than a half-century ago. The rise in prices affected downstream industries, such as in the creation of single- and multifamily residential construction, as well as transportation products, such as pallets.

Between April 2020 and April 2021, the superdisruption caused the price of lumber to increase, elevating the cost of an average new single-family house by $35,897 and the price of an average new multifamily house by $12,966.[3] During this period, product costs for a single-family home rose by 184 percent, with costs for a multifamily dwelling increasing by 190 percent. In addition, the average monthly rent for a new apartment rose by $119.[4] The result was the most significant increase in lumber prices since the post–World War II housing boom in the US.[5] In addition to housing costs, pandemic-triggered shift reductions, shutdowns, and lockdowns substantially reduced the production of wooden pallets, which nearly doubled from $9 to $15 and continued to rise into the third quarter of 2021.[6] The resulting pallet price escalation, in turn, increased the prices for all transported products, including fertilizer and other farm products.

The lumber industry's weaknesses revealed the need to focus on viability within a dynamic and responsive model that integrates and operationalizes adaption at different stages of a crisis. Viability focuses on the ability of any supply chain to preserve itself in an environment of change by redesigning structures and replanning business performance for long-term impacts.[7] Therefore, it must be an open system that allows adaptation to a new normal to survive radical changes in internal and external conditions.[8]

A dynamic and multidimensional construct of viability would seek the interaction and engagement of internal and external resources, including human labor, manufacturing processes, suppliers, transportation networks, and an effective communications structure. Economists Maciel Queiroz, Dmitry Ivanov, Alexandre Dolgui, and Samuel Fosso Wamba offer the following strategies for developing an effective operations and supply-chain-management business model that promotes viability.[9] Preparedness preallocates resources, incorporates distribution planning, and practices product diversification and substitution. An example is the use of simulation techniques employed to predict challenges in resource flows.

Adaption reallocates supply and demand and provides flexible production technologies to accommodate societal needs during a pandemic. An example is closely monitoring supply chains for masks, disinfectant spray, and ventilators and diversifying production when delays occur. Ripple effects attempt to control disruption propagations by modeling potential pandemic scenarios and the consequences of supply-chain structural dynamics. This strategy involves simulating interdependent supply chains to

Stacked kiln-dried lumber, Tianjin, China / Blaine Brownell

avoid a cascading effect in which a small problem becomes a much larger challenge downstream. Finally, sustainability integrates the recovery of capacities, the workforce, and logistical infrastructures while also forecasting pandemic propagations and ramping up the decision-making process. Sustainability aspires to long-term supply chain survivability with little or no disruptions.

Alexander Franco is an associate professor in the Neil Griffin College of Business at Arkansas State University.

In-Car Care

Ryan Hullinger

The limitations of healthcare delivery experienced during the pandemic have inspired a new model of mobile, user-oriented medicine.

——

Throughout the COVID-19 pandemic, we have hosted a series of charrettes exploring design solutions to meet the evolving needs of our healthcare clients and the communities they serve. We incubated many concepts through these events—addressing caregiver burnout, PPE shortages, mobile hospital construction, and the subject illustrated here, In-Car Care.

NBBJ developed the concept of In-Car Care in response to pandemic-driven changes in hospital and clinic visits. Noting that patients are now often directed (and prefer) to wait in their cars rather than traditional waiting rooms, we asked, "What if we didn't just relocate the patient-waiting experience into the car? What if we relocated the patient-care process in its entirety?"

Acknowledging that the cabin of a car is not the right setting for every type of care, we hypothesized that a considerable portion of low-acuity care could be delivered as well or better via an in-car platform—especially if the platform were purpose-designed around vehicular parameters. We have subsequently reviewed the hypothesis and the design approach with healthcare providers across the country and estimate that In-Car Care could be appropriate for up to 30 percent of the assessment and treatment procedures that currently occur in primary-, urgent-, and retail-care settings.

The purpose of this concept is not to replace telehealth or in-room visits. Instead, this strategy builds a bridge between these two platforms, offering unique advantages to both the patient and the provider. For the patient, the model provides increased convenience and patient agency: all activities occur within an environment that feels safe and user defined. Additionally, when compared to telehealth, the approach offers a significant increase in fidelity for assessing nuanced patient function (e.g., speech, eye tracking, cognition) and can benefit patients who struggle with telehealth technology or lack access to broadband internet at home. For the provider, the model offers streamlined patient throughput, reduced environmental cleaning load, and reduced construction and operating costs compared to conventional hospital and clinic structures.

Unlike traditional drive-through facilities based on serial-processing layouts, in our design, services are delivered to cars concurrently in multiple bays, providing parallel processing efficiency. The dimensions of the prefabricated bays are designed to provide caregivers with simultaneous access to every passenger in the car, with an overall module of sixty feet (eighteen meters), enabling alignment with the drive aisles and structures of existing parking garages and surface lots.

While the pandemic presents many challenges, it is also an opportunity to rethink the fundamentals of how and where care is provided. Ideas that enable our healthcare system to evolve, such as the In-Car Care concept, are critical to a future in which our healthcare infrastructure must be more resilient and adaptable than ever.

Ryan Hullinger is an architect and a partner at NBBJ.

NBBJ, rendering of the In-Car Care project showing multiple carports (top) and NBBJ, interior rendering of the In-Car Care project showing a patient consultation (bottom) / NBBJ

Home.Earth
Kasper Guldager Jensen

**Residential architecture must
be accessible to all and support
environmental health.**

—

Home.Earth is both a developer and
a real estate operator. It provides healthy
homes tailored to contemporary life patterns that are in balance with the planet,
and offers a community-focused live-
work platform.

We've all learned new ways of working
and communicating from the pandemic.
We've realized that we can spend less
time away from home. Most importantly,
social inequality has become more visible.
There has been a lot of stress for people in
marginalized communities. This condition
motivated us to establish a new real estate
model that caters to the whole society.

Our market is characterized by locations in major European cities with
measurable social inequalities. For those
who cannot pay, we offer a discount based
on a pay-what-you-can-afford approach.
Our site-selection guidelines and software
reveal a heat map of neighborhoods in
which lower-income individuals cannot
afford homes—that's where we build.

We consider three priorities: affordabil-
ity, livability, and sustainability. We have a
strong ambition to create climate-positive
buildings using the planetary boundaries
metrics established by the Stockholm
Resilience Center, which include climate
change, ozone depletion, and biosphere
integrity.[10] We emphasize three areas of
sustainability: attaining climate-positive
goals, achieving circular construction, and
increasing biodiversity. We establish a
benchmark of what exists on a site before
we build: biologists and entomologists
crawl around the site cataloging existing
species and generating a biodiversity
index. We work with established methods to realize a biodiversity net gain.
Our building system is based on off-site
modular construction, and we consider
buildings as material banks for stored
carbon. We are also developing material
passports, documents that inform how
best to apply materials that are not yet
commercially established.

During the pandemic, people realized
the importance of nature and that you
can't just isolate yourself in an urban environment. So nature became an integral
part of the design. We plan green spaces
to be as close to people as possible—adding dense foliage at the ground level with
intensive and extensive landscaping.
When such a strategy is not feasible on
a site, we build taller with green roofs
and walls. We map all existing trees and
reestablish the ones that need to move.
With planetary biodiversity in danger of
collapsing, we need to reverse the negative
trend of biodiversity loss: the aim should
be that the more we build, the more biodiversity is created.

*Kasper Guldager Jensen is an architect
and the cofounder of Home.Earth.*

Rendering of a Home.Earth multifamily-housing prototype (visuals: EFFEKT) (top) and interior rendering of a Home.Earth model residential unit (bottom) / Home.Earth

The Disorientation of Confinement

Lydia Kallipoliti

The pandemic invites a new understanding of interpersonal distance.

—

One question resonates in imagining the gradient end of the COVID-19 pandemic: What will happen when we can again move freely in space? Will the city be left behind? Will our memories—the heap of fragments of the spaces we occupied with intensity—mirror that which we will encounter?

This anxiety of reunifying the body with tangible space, as personal as it may be, marks prolonged confinement: a state of connected immobility, consistently zooming in and out of our physical coordinates. The delirium of the domestic sequestration of 2020 to 2022 marks not only the impossibility of returning to normality, as philosopher Slavoj Zizek vividly argues, but also profound disorientation and a rupture in the collective experience of public space.[11]

The pandemic state of blur that many writers and journalists describe is connected to the erosion of biorhythmic boundaries over time and how we exist in space. Cartesian positioning within a finite XYZ system has shifted to a spherical stereographic system linked to the self, relative to other spatial bodies. Determinate reference points have faded in our cognition, while a new order of moving bodies has emerged in an interrelational metric game of proximity and field interactions. With social distancing as the solitary reliable measure against the spread of COVID-19, cultural anthropologist Edward Hall's proxemic theory looms poignantly relevant.[12] While in 1963, Hall's attempts to define specific limits of personal space within a measurable notation system were critiqued as partly deterministic, the spatial order that Hall suggested—starting from the self as the origin point—exposes a resonant transactional modality of understanding space via distancing. There are many origin points in the space we inhabit, as the source of orientation is the self and the collective nucleus of bodies that coalesce as one. Bodies, therefore, enter a biotic *de*-coupling with their surroundings—or, as philosopher Quentin Meillassóux would say, a relational loss with context.[13] In order to navigate, bodies utilize themselves as parameters based on polar coordinates with vectors and distances rather than Cartesian coordinates. In this sense, pandemic space renders correlationism—or the need for embeddedness in the world—obsolete.

Philosopher Guy Debord and the situationists once argued that the city is no more than a fictionalized landscape that exists in many spatiotemporal dimensions according to individual recollections and reconstructions. Life, as Debord has stated, is replaced by its representation.[14] Yet this forward realization is now viciously descriptive of the present. Pervasive disorientation and multisensorial ubiquity now delineate the reconstruction of new geographies, mappings, and formal arrangements once freedom of movement is granted.

Lydia Kallipoliti is an assistant professor in the Irwin S. Chanin School of Architecture at the Cooper Union.

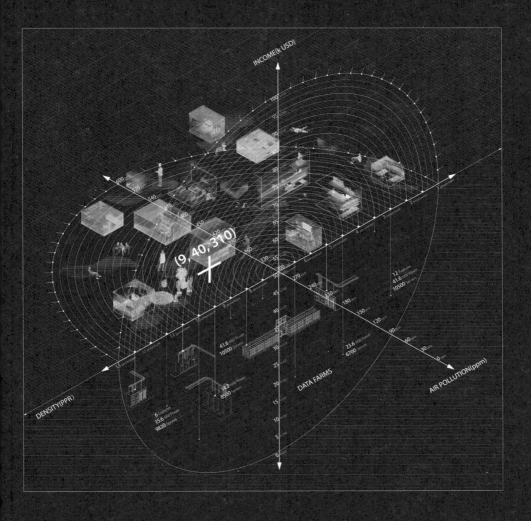

A diagram of interiors in a reconstructed topographical system of urban conditions based on income, air pollution, and density of people per square meter /
Lydia Kallipoliti, Xiaoxiao Zhao

Chapel of Healing

Li Hu and Huang Wenjing

**Evoking a pandemic-era architectural
sanctuary through poetry.** [15]

Returning to the solitude of inner self,
Echo of the sound of nature,
Resonate within the chamber.
With light and wind sweeping,
Time frozen.

Music arises,
Sound waves penetrate through the openings,
Touches and awakens the distant Great Wall,
Sleeping over the ridge for centuries.
From inside the instrument of music,
Reflecting off the surface of the folding
    concrete of the chamber,
Void of the chapel, a giant musical
    instrument.

Raindrops falling in through the oculus,
Dancing over the floor, becoming part
    of the symphony,
Merge and run through the chapel,
To join the creek that runs by.
Finding ways across the rocks,
    through the valley,
Under the Great Wall,
To the distant valleys beyond.

Like an ear gathering the voices of the sky,
Like a sanctuary for the souls,
Of the needed.
Like an ancient rock migrated here
    with the glaciers,
It comes to life with the materials of the land.
And it becomes part of the land again.
Enormous weight touches down gently,
In the valley, silently.
Letting the storms run by,
Sparrows flying through,
Insects undisturbed.

Monolithic and resilient,
To overcome the toughest challenge
    of nature
And test of time.
Consuming the least amount of resources,
And accommodating the most
    generous gatherings,
It welcomes all curiosity and passion;
And the search for the collective reflection
On the delicate balance we must orchestrate
Between us and the environment that
    we must survive
In and together.

*Li Hu and Huang Wenjing are founding
partners of OPEN Architecture.*

Open Architecture, Chapel of Sound, Chengde, Hebei Province, China, 2021 / Jonathan Leijonhufvud

Metabolic Hybrids

Clare Lyster

COVID-19 has motivated closer connections between agriculture and data systems.

——

Two seemingly isolated effects of the pandemic will have lasting influences on the city. The first is the strain the pandemic exercised over food supply chains. Visions of empty supermarkets are still vivid after panic buying, partly the result of disruptions in the harvesting, processing, and distribution of food systems. In addition, there were bottlenecks in meatpacking facilities and heavy losses in production, especially in the major fruit and vegetable growing areas in the US. Covid exposed challenges in contemporary food flows that were already under scrutiny prepandemic—long distances between food production and consumption, large multinational food conglomerates controlling global supply chains, and a reduction in the variety of foods for greater production efficiencies, among others. We've learned the need for alternative agricultural strategies for a meaningful and healthier approach to food security and food repair moving forward as crises—from climate change to contagion—continue to threaten urban areas.

The second is the overwhelming increase in our dependency on digital infrastructure in everyday activities, from virtual meetings to e-commerce and streaming media, not to mention Covid tracking apps and digital health certifications that will only continue to be useful as other pandemics loom. It's no surprise that the large IT companies have fared well during COVID-19—Apple, Amazon, Facebook, and Alphabet (Google) all reporting record profits and all included in the top eight most profitable companies during the pandemic.

More information means more data centers to store information and more energy to sustain them. Ireland, one of Europe's largest data storage hubs, is a case in point. By 2030, the country plans to dedicate 30 percent of its electrical energy to IT—an industry whose hyperscale facilities can use as much power as a midsize city. Moreover, these data centers release vast amounts of warm exhaust air into the atmosphere after it has been used to cool the servers within. This accumulation could be more productively redeployed elsewhere with some planning.[16]

The modern city was premised on the separation and isolation of systems in the logic that mono-functioning infrastructures are more efficient. However, the pandemic has proved that the hybridization of previously separated programs (e.g., home-office, home-school, park-yoga) is a viable rescripting of urban space that will motivate the hybridization of larger-scale natural and sociotechnical systems, such as metabolic exchanges between agricultural production and data infrastructure.

Data Farm#1 is a speculative proposal that combines data storage, vertical farming, vending, and a bus shelter into a single node that is distributed throughout the city.[17] The heat from data-storage racks is transferred to modular vertical-farming units on the roof of the bus stop to produce fruit, microgreens, and vegetables that are picked by robots and dropped into an on-site vending machine for public consumption. The prototype highlights symbiosis as one of the long-term spatial transformations of Covid in which more resilient adjacencies between nature,

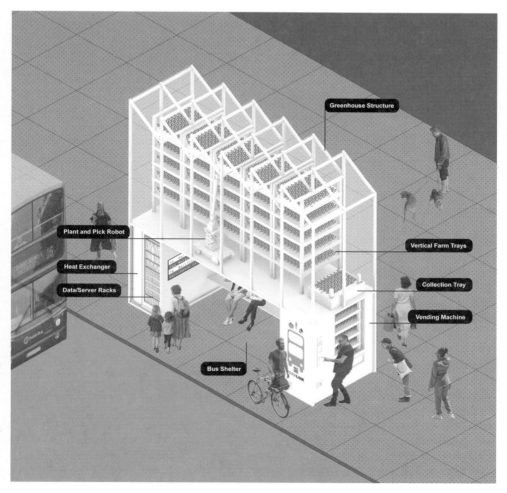

CLUAA, Farm Link axonometric diagram, 2022 /
CLUAA / Clare Lyster with Charles Lafon

technology, and culture, what political scientist Timothy Luke refers to as cyber-organic ecologies, emerge to immunize the built environment from further upheaval.[18] As this work indicates, metabolic hybridization has become the new normal.

Clare Lyster is a professor in the School of Architecture at the University of Illinois at Chicago and a principal of Clare Lyster Urbanism and Architecture (CLUAA).

Quiet Casualties

Rebecca McLaughlan and Emma Kirby

**What has been lost in the race
to protect palliative-care patients
from the pandemic?**

———

Media images and headlines have focused on the heartbreak of dying with/from Covid—isolated, removed from loved ones, and without human contact. In contrast, those receiving palliative care have hitherto mainly gone unnoticed. In Australia, the number of patients hospitalized with COVID-19 remained lower than the scale of suffering endured elsewhere. This circumstance provided a unique window into the everyday consequences of pandemic-related restrictions on the experience of palliative care—the quiet forgoing of things previously taken for granted—that, for those affected, have by no means been quotidian.

Palliative care is characterized by a distinct philosophy that foregrounds the provision of emotional and physical comfort to patients and their families. Critical to facilitating such comfort are architectural affordances that encourage round-the-clock visitation, opportunities for social connection and support, and access to green space. But the pandemic has necessitated various restrictions implemented to keep people safe. Consequently, some patients remain alone or in the presence of a staff member, while others are allowed a single "approved visitor" at their bedside. Social spaces, including shared courtyard gardens, have been locked and designated off-limits for months on end. Reluctant to being separated from families, patients nearing the end of life have remained at home in numbers not previously seen in Australia. Such changes raise important questions about the emotional costs of these losses,

prompting much debate around how to better support people in palliative care.

Various planning arrangements have enabled and constrained experiences of pandemic palliative care. Single-occupancy rooms allowed fewer interruptions to visitation. Ground-floor rooms with external access also allowed safer conditions for families and enabled pets to visit in some settings. In other locations, however, external access proved an impediment to managing visitation, increasing staff workload due to the need to monitor multiple entry and exit pathways. This, among many other examples, shows the limits to what we can achieve through built solutions. Greater investment in telehealth and services to support care in the home is needed, while the connectivity offered by technology has never been more critical. The end of life typically brings families together, and while a video call is no substitute for the intimacy of physical proximity, designing to ensure sufficient access to technology within healthcare spaces is vital. How comfort and connection are experienced has become a key indicator of success or failure in response to pandemic conditions.

Rebecca McLaughlan is an Australian Research Council DECRA research fellow and a senior lecturer in architecture at the School of Architecture and Design, University of Sydney.

Emma Kirby is a UNSW Scientia Associate Professor of sociology in the Faculty of Arts, Design and Architecture at the University of New South Wales.

Ryder Architecture, Prince and Princess of Wales Hospice, Glasgow, Scotland, 2019 / Keith Hunter

Stay-at-home Stress

Amelyn Ng

Many families, such as the residents of Houston's Fifth Ward, encountered significant challenges during the coronavirus lockdown.

——

Throughout COVID-19's myriad lockdowns and stay-at-home orders, the world was forced to shelter in place in the space of one's home, for days or months on end. While stay-at-home narratives often paint an easy picture of working from home, this was not the reality for residents who were essential workers or had little access to amenities, such as home internet, air-conditioning, food storage, drinkable tap water, or backyards where children could play safely beyond the confines of the home.

As the pandemic raged on, it became apparent that home stress was disproportionately experienced and had spatial, social, and environmental dimensions. What pandemic reports often fail to convey adequately is the struggle of domestic life: large intergenerational families quarantining under one roof with a single bathroom; an essential worker shedding her scrubs nightly in an apartment-entry vestibule; a mother and three children waiting out a four-day blackout. Stories of resilience also tend to go unnoticed: how the shaded porch became a key outdoor space for family meals or respite from children; how the living room was converted into a hair salon; how a pod of care workers rotated homes for game nights throughout the pandemic.

These narratives were documented in *Stay-at-home Stress*, a spatial survey seeking to identify the material impacts of lockdown on families in Houston's Fifth Ward.[19] With the Fifth Ward Center for Urban Transformation, my graduate assistants and I conducted qualitative video interviews with sixteen residents and translated their lockdown experiences into annotated plan drawings.[20] For many of these households, living rooms doubled as bedrooms. Kitchen tables became school desks. Parks and washaterias were vital neighborhood services. Storm-damaged roofs and floors were self-repaired while waiting for building maintenance. Indoor heat stress emerged as a top concern: residents obscured windows with cardboard, foil, and heavy drapes to mitigate the summer heat.[21] This is a significant matter, considering that Houston saw extreme one-hundred-degree summer days in 2020. In a warming climate, the thermally regulated interior becomes a fundamental human right alongside equitable access to housing. Ultimately, the health crisis is not an isolated event but is enmeshed with longer-term environmental and social inequalities. These unequal relations manifest physically in the space of the home, and the voices of their residents must be heard and supported—in or out of a lockdown.[22]

Amelyn Ng is an assistant professor in the Department of Architecture at the Rhode Island School of Design.

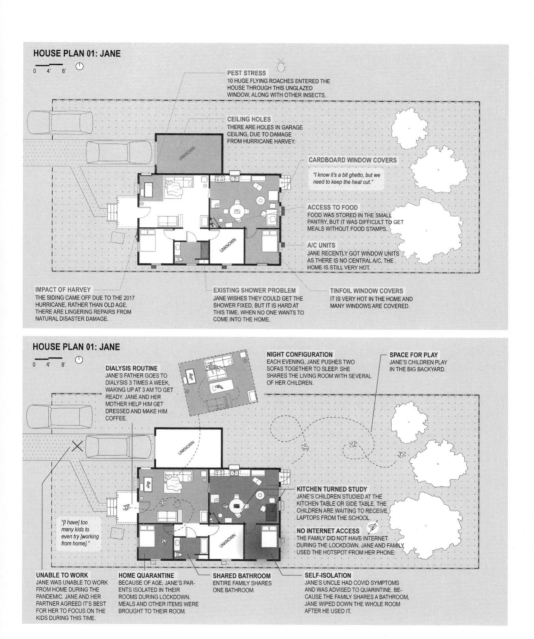

HOUSE PLAN 01: JANE

0   4'   8'

PEST STRESS
10 HUGE FLYING ROACHES ENTERED THE HOUSE THROUGH THIS UNGLAZED WINDOW, ALONG WITH OTHER INSECTS.

CEILING HOLES
THERE ARE HOLES IN GARAGE CEILING, DUE TO DAMAGE FROM HURRICANE HARVEY.

CARDBOARD WINDOW COVERS
"I know it's a bit ghetto, but we need to keep the heat out."

ACCESS TO FOOD
FOOD WAS STORED IN THE SMALL PANTRY, BUT IT WAS DIFFICULT TO GET MEALS WITHOUT FOOD STAMPS.

A/C UNITS
JANE RECENTLY GOT WINDOW UNITS AS THERE IS NO CENTRAL A/C. THE HOME IS STILL VERY HOT.

IMPACT OF HARVEY
THE SIDING CAME OFF DUE TO THE 2017 HURRICANE, RATHER THAN OLD AGE. THERE ARE LINGERING REPAIRS FROM NATURAL DISASTER DAMAGE.

EXISTING SHOWER PROBLEM
JANE WISHES THEY COULD GET THE SHOWER FIXED, BUT IT IS HARD AT THIS TIME, WHEN NO ONE WANTS TO COME INTO THE HOME.

TINFOIL WINDOW COVERS
IT IS VERY HOT IN THE HOME AND MANY WINDOWS ARE COVERED.

HOUSE PLAN 01: JANE

0   4'   8'

DIALYSIS ROUTINE
JANE'S FATHER GOES TO DIALYSIS 3 TIMES A WEEK, WAKING UP AT 3 AM TO GET READY. JANE AND HER MOTHER HELP HIM GET DRESSED AND MAKE HIM COFFEE.

NIGHT CONFIGURATION
EACH EVENING, JANE PUSHES TWO SOFAS TOGETHER TO SLEEP. SHE SHARES THE LIVING ROOM WITH SEVERAL OF HER CHILDREN.

SPACE FOR PLAY
JANE'S CHILDREN PLAY IN THE BIG BACKYARD.

KITCHEN TURNED STUDY
JANE'S CHILDREN STUDIED AT THE KITCHEN TABLE OR SIDE TABLE. THE CHILDREN ARE WAITING TO RECEIVE LAPTOPS FROM THE SCHOOL.

NO INTERNET ACCESS
THE FAMILY DID NOT HAVE INTERNET DURING THE LOCKDOWN. JANE AND FAMILY USED THE HOTSPOT FROM HER PHONE.

"[I have] too many kids to even try [working from home]."

UNABLE TO WORK
JANE WAS UNABLE TO WORK FROM HOME DURING THE PANDEMIC. JANE AND HER PARTNER AGREED IT'S BEST FOR HER TO FOCUS ON THE KIDS DURING THIS TIME.

HOME QUARANTINE
BECAUSE OF AGE, JANE'S PARENTS ISOLATED IN THEIR ROOMS DURING LOCKDOWN. MEALS AND OTHER ITEMS WERE BROUGHT TO THEIR ROOM.

SHARED BATHROOM
ENTIRE FAMILY SHARES ONE BATHROOM.

SELF-ISOLATION
JANE'S UNCLE HAD COVID SYMPTOMS AND WAS ADVISED TO QUARANTINE. BECAUSE THE FAMILY SHARES A BATHROOM, JANE WIPED DOWN THE WHOLE ROOM AFTER HE USED IT.

Amelyn Ng with Carrie Li and Carolyn Francis, site plan (top) and house plan (bottom) developed based on an interview with "Jane," showing sources of environmental and social stress. *Stay-at-home Stress* survey, Houston, Texas, 2020 / Amelyn Ng

Colab-19

Alejandro Saldarriaga and German Bahamon

A new, resource-aware model of architectural practice has found success during the pandemic.

———

The notion that crisis leads to opportunity might be correct in many scenarios. However, traditional architectural practice has not responded adequately to global socioeconomic challenges throughout history. Are we so dependent on the economic drivers of our society that we can't accommodate as a profession and design appropriately for the reoccurring crises of our contemporary world? We argue that traditional practice and construction methods in our discipline are outdated and cannot adapt to the everyday emergencies of modern society. To support this hypothesis, we, as Colab-19, offer the design ethos that has allowed us to create an architectural practice in the middle of a global crisis.

The start of the COVID-19 pandemic led to unprecedented socioeconomic turmoil throughout the world, and Colombia's capital, Bogotá, felt these effects fully. Since Bogotá is a place where most of the population does not have the opportunity to work from home, we noticed the need for a new type of space that would allow economic reactivation. However, designing in an environment in which neither institutions nor private entities had any means of funding a new architectural intervention made us realize that there is a flaw in how we traditionally imagine architecture. This recognition forced us to develop a design method of expediently reusing resources that are part of our daily urban environment. This design logic came to differentiate us from other designers proposing ideas for postpandemic reactivation and allowed us to build four

projects in less than a year. These projects used infrastructure systems that are part of daily life and allowed us to question traditional building methods and how we inhabit our cities. Furthermore, through our reflection of the flaws of contemporary praxis, we realized that we don't need a physical space to operate as an architecture practice—and to this day, the two of us have never met physically.

We are constantly pushing to reapply our design ethos to different scales, and we firmly believe that the design approach used to create our projects is not exclusive to the pandemic crisis. We live in a time when the problems of mass migration, climate change, and social inequity are continually increasing. Therefore, there is a need for a new informal, responsive type of postpandemic architecture that questions the rigid methods of traditional architectural practice. Consequently, by applying an approach to design that is more resourceful, adaptable, and responsive to the existing physical context, the architecture profession will be able to accommodate the periodic crises of our modern world more adequately.

Alejandro Saldarriaga and German Bahamon are architects and the cofounders of Colab-19.

Colab-19, Alhambra's Cross, a temporary open-air church created for pandemic Easter in Bogota, Colombia, 2021 / Alberto Roa

Multisensory Wayfinding

Joel Sanders, Seb Choe, Hansel Bauman,
Magda Mostafa, and Eron Friedlaender

The heath and mobility needs of marginalized groups should be central concerns in postpandemic design.
—

The aftermath of the pandemic will irrevocably change the design of the built environment in the same way that 9/11 changed the way we think about building security. There will be a demand for higher standards to maintain health and hygiene in public and private buildings, with a need to consider the challenges and barriers this poses to some vulnerable groups. This dovetails with the recognition that intersecting marginalized communities, including the poor, elderly, disabled, and people of color, were disproportionately impacted by the pandemic.

We must imagine equitable postpandemic public spaces as a natural extension of the mission to create safe and accessible buildings that promote equity, health, and well-being. With the spread of the coronavirus disease, all of us have become noncompliant bodies: hyperaware and often anxious about how to maneuver safely within once familiar but now disabling spaces. This attentiveness affords us a new appreciation for the lived experience of those for whom such exclusion and noncompliance is a daily occurrence. For people to feel safe and connected, they need public spaces to be purposely designed to minimize distractions caused by environmental stressors induced by disorienting spaces and overstimulation by noise, light, and crowd activity that risks unintended contact with other people or surfaces.

We are learning lessons about how the built environment can provide multisensory cues that enable spatial orientation, agency, and a sense of security in public spaces through studying the three marginalized communities: individuals requiring assisted mobility, the deaf, and the autistic. Many commonalities exist among the adaptive strategies from each of these populations, which can be applied to the design of public spaces for enhanced spatial orientation and safety for most users within today's spatial paradigm, placing health and equity central to all design.

Unobstructed paths of travel allow people with mobility challenges to maneuver with limited potential obstacles. Other recommendations include smooth surfaces, ideally wide enough for pairs of wheelchairs moving in opposite directions to pass one another, avoiding abrupt level changes, and alternatives to deep carpets and other rough textures that may collect debris and impede movement.

Architecture attuned to deaf sensibilities includes wide, barrier-free circulation pathways to allow adequate space for interlocutors to engage safely in a signed conversation while walking; circular group-seating arrangements permit clear, equitable sightlines between all participants; and glare-free, diffused lighting and wall colors that contrast with human skin tones and reduce eyestrain and sharpen visual acuity.

The spatial needs of autistic and neurodiverse people may be met by sequencing spaces in a predictable way to flow from one activity to the next, grouping functions into high-stimulus and low-stimulus zones separated by transition spaces to allow individuals to recalibrate between different experiences. Designs may also reduce environmental stress by modulating acoustics to minimize background noise and reverberation and controlling light-level intensity, color, and glare. Overall, making public spaces intuitive, with clear signage and a readable organization of seating, reception, entrances, exits, and corridors, to promote independence in navigating new environments.

Multisensory Wayfinding is a work in progress and reflects our conviction that social equity and public health are mutually reinforcing propositions. Designing through the lens of diversity promises to be a catalyst for creativity that can ultimately yield safe, accessible, and hygienic spaces for all of us. As autism design consultant Magda Mostafa reminds us: "When you design with a mindfulness of the extremities, you invariably benefit the entire range of the spectrum." [23]

Tactile and visual signage on a train platform / Lisanto 李奕良

Joel Sanders is the principal of Joel Sanders Architect, a professor in the practice in the School of Architecture at Yale University, and the director of MIXdesign.

Seb Choe is an associate director of MIXdesign.

Hansel Bauman is a recognized leader in the development of deaf architecture, the author of DeafSpace Design Guidelines (2010), and the former director of Campus Design and Planning at Gallaudet University.

Magda Mostafa is a leading autism expert and the author of the Autism ASPECTSS Design Index (2015), the first research-based design framework for autism worldwide.

Eron Friedlaender is a professor of clinical pediatrics in the Perelman School of Medicine at the University of Pennsylvania and an attending physician in the Division of Emergency Medicine at the Children's Hospital of Philadelphia.

Redesigning Schools

Nicola Springer

The pandemic reinforced the imperative to improve indoor air quality and site design in schools.

Before COVID-19 brought into stark light the socioeconomic and environmental disparities within and around our educational facilities, school designers were addressing a paradigm shift that was taking place regarding educational pedagogy, architecture, and sustainable design. In many ways, Covid was the catalyst—twenty years into the twenty-first century—that emphasized the push for advances in school design and education delivery that we can no longer ignore.

Sustainable design platforms like the U.S. Green Building Council's LEED for Schools have raised awareness about indoor air quality. Evidence-based design studies have elevated the importance of natural daylight and outdoor views, registering correlated student performance in reading and math. These reports have highlighted concerns about the time children spend indoors and in overcrowded classrooms. In addition, psychological and behavioral studies have emphasized that physical activity and time spent outdoors are restorative to overall student health and well-being. So, when public health experts acknowledged during the pandemic that fresh air, open windows, and outdoor environments are simple ways to keep COVID-19 transmission at bay, school designers like me felt emboldened and vindicated.

Given the health benefits of outdoor learning, we must take advantage of this free resource. Just as we design and program interior spaces to foster creativity and support multiple learning and teaching styles, we must take the same care to create stimulating, engaging, and restorative outdoor spaces. Air movement is critical for successful outdoor learning. During the pandemic, teachers shifted students outdoors as a last resort; however, we must consider the microclimate we create around our buildings during the site-design phase. Our responsibility as architects is to assess how our schools can contribute to a restorative and positive learning environment. We can accomplish this goal by siting buildings to take advantage of prevailing winds, providing breezeways and porches to create in-between spaces that channel air and provide shade. In addition, we must consider other challenges to quality outdoor spaces, especially in urban areas. How do you buffer the site from street noise? Can you filter air pollution, manage relentless parking lots, and solve flooding? How can you use plant life, trees, and grasses to mitigate these negative effects?

Ultimately, one of the most important revelations from the pandemic is that our public schools are our communities' hearts, souls, and literal futures. We ask so much of our schools, and we should design to optimize the services they are expected to provide. During the pandemic, "pod schools" allowed families of means to escape the city and learn in and from nature. We must provide such opportunities to all students and prioritize the health and well-being of all our schools, indoors and out. Only then can we create healthy and vibrant educational ecosystems, where young people can thrive in body, spirit, and mind.

Nicola Springer is an architect and an executive vice president at Kirksey Architecture.

Kirksey Architecture, Norman-Sims Elementary School, Austin, Texas, 2020 / Shau Lin Hon

From Virus to Fungus

Marc Swackhamer, Blair Satterfield,
Matt Hayes, and Jacob Taswell

Employing natural organisms to transform PPE waste into new materials is an untapped opportunity.

—

Globally, we use sixty-five billion medical-grade gloves every month. The monthly tally for face masks is 129 billion, or 3 million per minute.[24] Face masks, gloves, wipes, and other PPE contain plastic fibers, primarily polypropylene, that linger in the environment for decades, breaking down into smaller microplastics and nanoplastics. A single face mask can release 173,000 microfibers per day into the ocean. What can we reasonably do with all this plastic? We might look to the humble mushroom for answers.

In her recent book *The Mushroom at the End of the World: On the Possibility of Life in Capitalist Ruins*, Anna Tsing writes about the matsutake mushroom. In the introduction, she remarks,

> Matsutake is the most valuable mushroom in the world—and a weed that grows in human-disturbed forests across the northern hemisphere. Through its ability to nurture trees, matsutake helps forests to grow in daunting places. It is also an edible delicacy in Japan, where it sometimes commands astronomical prices. In all its contradictions, matsutake offers insights into areas far beyond just mushrooms and addresses a crucial question: what manages to live in the ruins we have made? [25]

We already reuse PPE to make concrete, insulation, raw plastic pellets, 3D printable fiber, flooring, and artificial turf.[26] But this manufacturing requires additional energy input and still poses the same environmental challenges as traditional processes. What if we think more disruptively?

What if we purposefully offer PPE back to nature rather than passively hope nature will someday take care of our ruins?

To this end, we might consider the fungus *Pestalotiopis microspora*. While conducting research in Ecuador in 2010, students from Yale University discovered strains of the fungus that could digest and break down polyurethane plastic. These strains can survive on plastic alone.[27] Two other species of mushrooms, *Ganoderma lucidum* and *Pleurotus ostreatus*, can grow into a strong, sustainable building material called mycelium.[28] A genetic hybrid of these mushroom species could transform discarded pandemic waste (i.e., PPE) into a nutrient that grows new building materials (i.e., mycelium). This renewable, grown material could then address other pressing global crises, like housing scarcity.

If we as designers can assume the role of material managers and not simply material shapers, we can positively impact the built environment by using surplus to address scarcity. Working this way necessitates the erasure of disciplinary boundaries that limit our thinking and further entrench old habits. We might start by partnering with our fellow planetary organisms.

Mushrooms sprouting on a nurse log, British Columbia, Canada / Blair Satterfield

Marc Swackhamer is a professor and chair of the Department of Architecture at the University of Colorado Denver.

Blair Satterfield is chair of the architecture program and an associate professor in the School of Architecture and Landscape Architecture at the University of British Columbia.

Matt Hayes is a research assistant and graduate student in the Department of Architecture at the University of Colorado Denver.

Jacob Taswell is a research assistant and graduate student in the Department of Architecture at the University of Colorado Denver.

The Archipelago

Francis Wilmore

The postpandemic workplace should represent a radical departure from the traditional office.

———

The Archipelago is a novel workplace that incorporates elements of a resort, providing collaborative meeting spaces that also fulfill remote workers' longing for a relaxing vacation after months of lockdown. Since the beginning of the COVID-19 pandemic, as frontline workers routinely donned and doffed their personal protective equipment, office employees exchanged daily business attire for more casual work-from-home outfits. The design of a new kind of workplace was inspired by the need to address immediate social distancing challenges while looking to a viable future for office work.

The Archipelago is a collection of private islands for outdoor coworking housed under a cabana-shade structure. Occupants doff their traditional business attire and are sanitized before entering the workspace. The concept's plan consists of three island rings of workspaces sized according to a six-foot social-distance bubble. The islands are equipped with furniture specifically designed to separate coworkers at the recommended six-foot increments. The islands range in size to accommodate groups of two to six people and are physically separated by canals rather than the typical yet less effective distancing stickers placed on floors. The islands can be used collectively as an open-office concept, or spaces can be subdivided using water curtains for privacy. The water curtains may also be used to aggregate chains of islands for larger groups.

The concept provides a safe coworking space that addresses society's significantly changed attitudes toward workplace design.

With the coronavirus-motivated shift to telecommuting, we must consider what the postpandemic world should be. Why would individuals remain sequestered in their homes—or even stay in their hometowns—when it is possible to work from anywhere? The Archipelago concept addresses the immediate need for a socially distanced, safe office environment while considering a new model of the workplace.

Francis Wilmore is an architect and the director of design at KKT Architects.

**KKT Architects, rendering (top) and site rendering (bottom) of the
Archipelago project** / KKT Architects

Chapter Five

THE PUBLIC REALM

Pandemic-responsive cities, landscapes, and infrastructure that support public health and environmental justice

W hen the first pandemic stay-at-home measures were enacted in spring 2020, the world became much smaller for those not in frontline occupations. Sequestered at home and relying on the internet for work, school, and food delivery was curiously reminiscent of the kind of existence proposed by architects Toyo Ito and Kazuyo Sejima in their 1980s urban-nomad dwellings. These conceptual one-room structures provided spaces for sleeping, dressing, eating, and connecting to digital media—long before the internet was widely used.[1] This proposed independent lifestyle had a dark side, however, which was reflected in Ito's assessment of modern society's increasing disassociation from place: "The communication which was once deeply rooted in an area or in a local community has lost its significance," he wrote in "Architecture in a Simulated City."[2] "What is thriving in our cities is based on a network of instantaneous, ephemeral, and unspecific but numerous media which deny a physical distance."

Once people began to reemerge from their homes in summer 2020, they encountered a very different public realm, one largely devoid of life, with many buildings now off-limits. As streets repopulated, people became fearful of cities due to their high densities and probability of virus transmission. In addition, the relatively small footprints and high rents of urban residences inspired an exodus among remote workers with means. According to one report, large US metro areas witnessed 600,000 people move to midsize cities and 740,000 to small towns between March 2020 to March 2021.[3] For these urban emigrants, the decision to move was not only based on economics but also a pandemic-influenced reassessment of priorities. According to urban studies theorist Richard Florida: "People are asking deep questions about how and where they want to live."[4] Florida called the phenomenon "the great unmooring"; others called it "the great pandemic migration."[5]

The urban exodus prompted a renewed consideration for sparsely populated settlement models that could rely upon the internet—not population density—for connectivity. "Rather than the Radiant City of glass towers looming over copious parks prophesied by Le Corbusier, we are likely to end up with urban centers more like Frank Lloyd Wright's Broadacre City concept: vast expanses of low-lying private homes connected by both roads and the Internet," wrote urban studies scholar Joel Kotkin.[6] Wright's model city was intended to be a physical manifestation of democratic ideals, providing individuals with more space and opportunity than traditional urban centers characterized by concentrated power and social stratification.[7] Adopting a pandemic mindset of reducing communicable disease vectors, Broadacre City's dispersed population and ample open spaces would appear to be inherently desirable characteristics.

And yet inhabitants of exurban areas were shown to fare worse during the pandemic than those in urban centers. According to sociologist David Peters, rural communities in the US demonstrated greater vulnerability to the coronavirus disease than urban ones.[8] These populations experience higher per capita risk factors based on reduced access to healthcare infrastructure, an older average age, and a higher prevalence of chronic health conditions. Exurban areas also tend to be the sites of large collective facilities, such as nursing homes, prisons, and meatpacking plants, which have been shown to accelerate the spread of infectious diseases. Studies of COVID-19 vulnerability thus revealed far greater susceptibility in micropolitan, semirural, and rural communities than in metropolitan centers.[9]

Cities are fundamentally important for reasons beyond pandemic resilience. As economists Edward Glaeser and David Cutler describe, "Ultimately, cities will remain strong because they are places that allow us to exercise our deeply human love of personal connection."[10] This yearning for connection is one not fully satisfied by remote communication. The desire for in-person interaction and tangible experiences is evident in the growing crowds at street cafes (or "streateries"), city parks, outdoor sporting events, and musical performances. During the pandemic, many municipalities temporarily converted city streets into pedestrian zones and sidewalks into restaurants— changes residents now want to make permanent.[11] While this trend has the conceptual advantages of encouraging pedestrian mobility and social equity, care must be taken to avoid possible negative consequences, such as excluding street vendors and the homeless from an increasingly privatized and demographically homogeneous public realm.

An element of the designed environment that revealed its critical importance during the pandemic is the urban park.

When the first stay-at-home measures were relaxed in 2020, parks became a priority destination for city dwellers. According to one survey that characterized the urban park as a pandemic "lifesaver," respondents described tranquility, access to nature, and "awe" as the primary reasons for visiting urban green spaces.[12] The reminder of the necessity of parks and open spaces allows one to reconsider priorities in land-use planning. Nearly a third of urban land in the US today consists of paved streets and parking lots; meanwhile, the area devoted to parks is only 15 percent.[13] In a Lincoln Institute of Land Policy survey, respondents indicated a desire to increase access to parks and reinforced the role of parks in maintaining physical and mental health.[14]

Given the necessity of health, designers of buildings and spaces must find ways to navigate the inherently contradictory set of public health priorities in pandemic times and beyond. Isolation is the obvious form of controlling the spread of infectious illness—as seen in the practices of quarantine, social distancing, and the erection of physical barriers. However, isolation also can increase disease due to the negative psychological impacts of loneliness. In one study, isolated individuals were shown to be three times more susceptible to virus infection after exposure than those who maintained many social ties.[15] In another, isolated subjects were revealed to be two-to-three times more likely to die within a nine-year period than socially connected individuals.[16] Such findings reinforce the vital role cities and public spaces have in bringing people together as a matter of health. As we consider how the built environment can respond to future pandemics, one of the most significant challenges for architects, designers, and planners will be how to create spaces that limit the spread of infectious disease while maintaining in-person connections.

The contributions in this chapter address significant coronavirus-related issues and opportunities in the public realm. The essays span the gamut of relevant design topics, including urban furniture, streetscapes, city parks, mobility infrastructure, and public lands. Special attention is paid to issues of social justice and to questions of cities' and parks' contributions to individual health and well-being.

Reconsider the Street

Sara Jensen Carr

Reimagine streetscapes to prioritize people over vehicles.

——

Throughout urban history, streets have been both laboratories and battlegrounds in combating the particular illnesses of their eras. For example, streets were identified as the primary source of cholera and yellow-fever outbreaks during the Industrial Revolution. Linked to the ingestion of polluted water, the outbreaks were the results of the palpable filth of waste piled on the sides of swampy mud roads and spurred engineers, architects, and municipal agencies to combine forces and install miles of underground sewage, pave streets, and employ new sanitation departments to keep them clean, all within a couple of decades. However, the resulting optimization of transportation infrastructure in the United States—most often put into the service of moving white middle- and upper-class workers to the suburbs as quickly as possible to escape the perceived growing ills of the city—occurred at the cost of the health of communities of color, who were left to breathe the exhaust of automobiles and suffer the effects of urban disinvestment.

During the initial chaos of the COVID-19 pandemic, the de-optimization of streets revealed the possibilities of healthier cities. Drastic changes in commuting patterns left streets and parking lots empty. Photos of these voids became the preeminent image of the early days of the pandemic, reflecting anxieties about whether this image signaled the much-discussed, but never to materialize, "end of cities." Soon, though, many cities temporarily reclaimed these spaces to expand parks, pedestrian thoroughfares, and bike paths or granted parking spaces for restaurants to provide outdoor seating. However, if "streateries" in high-end neighborhoods are the pandemic's only lasting effects on the urban landscape, it would be a drastically missed opportunity to reprioritize people instead of vehicles in the public realm. How might we instead reimagine the street to extend open space, social commons, and mass transportation to neighborhoods that suffered the brunt of their health effects throughout the twentieth century? In the nineteenth century, technological innovation and a significant allocation of labor transformed the street to eliminate real environmental hazards and perceived moral ones. After the weaponization of roads to isolate and poison vulnerable communities of color in the twentieth century—the same neighborhoods that suffered disproportionate rates of COVID-19 mortality—our charge in the twenty-first century is more complex but no less urgent: to leverage our attendant resources and ingenuity to transform a landscape of harm into one of healing.

Sara Jensen Carr is an assistant professor of architecture at Northeastern University and the author of **The Topography of Wellness: How Health and Disease Shaped the American Landscape** *(2021).*

Boramae Park, Sindaebang-dong, Seoul, South Korea / Daniel Bernard

We Need Our Parks

Anna Cawrse

The intensified use of public parks reinforces their fundamental importance and points to new design strategies for urban landscapes.

—

While 2020 was a time of complete uncertainty, it was also a time of clarity. As a society, we started to understand the importance of our community, the value of creative outlets, and the new roles parks and the public realm would play in our lives. Urban parks and plazas became our living rooms, kitchens, day cares, restaurants, and the arena for social connection after months of isolation. Many of these public spaces had previously been underutilized and taken for granted for years. Suddenly, small pocket parks were a neighborhood destination, and larger parks were havens for entire cities. However, stresses like business closures put pressure on cities' finances, leaving some public spaces to fend for themselves. From now on, we don't want to create a short-term solution for a decades-long funding and design problem.

Although we as designers can't instantly influence municipal-funding structures, our design interventions can balance the new, immediate demands on our parks with longevity. Now is the time to respond to the intensified use of parks in the design and construction of new parks, the renovation of existing spaces, and, ultimately, visions for long-term park maintenance. Our designs must balance the need for active programs (i.e., the "entertaining" spaces) with smaller outdoor rooms that provide a much-needed respite from our busy, plugged-in life. A study reported in the *Guardian* in 2019 shows that a two-hour "dose" of nature each week has significant health benefits.[17]

So how do we design and retrofit our parks to meet the demands of our cities? Public spaces must balance a rewilding approach with one that can support more highly programmed spaces. Rewilding is a two-step design strategy that identifies areas within our parks where we can limit turf, reintroduce native flora, and increase biodiversity, which reduces irrigation and the need for herbicides and pesticides. In tow with this approach, we need to engage and educate the public on the ecological benefits of rewilding parks to show them the value of this strategy. However, we must also educate ourselves as designers by listening to public feedback. Not everyone wants something "wild," and in many places, this style can be viewed as unsafe and neglected. An optimal approach is to implement what landscape architect Joan Nassauer calls "cues to care"—creating purposeful borders, such as mowed edges around native plantings.[18] We can carefully curate a landscape that meets the program desires of a community, reduces pressures on the environment, and ultimately requires less maintenance.[19]

Heading into the endemic, we will continue to look to our parks as critical spaces to connect with nature and as places for gatherings of all shapes and sizes. Parks are not a nicety within our cities; they are essential pieces of infrastructure within the urban fabric. Therefore, we must design parks to be flexible, resilient, and capable of evolving.

Anna Cawrse is a landscape architect and a principal of Sasaki.

Sasaki, rendering of the Greenwood Community Park Master Plan and Implementation in Baton Rouge, Louisiana, expected completion 2022 / Sasaki Associates

Mini Block City
Yung Ho Chang

Organizing urban fabric with micro-scaled blocks creates a pedestrian-friendly environment that is easy to manage from a public health perspective.

———

In recent years, before COVID-19 broke out, our practice, Atelier FCJZ, completed an industrial park in the Jiading District of Shanghai, which has small city blocks measuring 131 feet (40 meters) per side with streets 33 feet (10 meters) wide in between. The intention was to bring a more human scale to urban spaces so that people might once again enjoy urban life, engaging in activities (e.g., taking a stroll after lunch). The project has thus far been a commercial success, well received by tenants and end users.

When the raging pandemic made the world critical about urbanity, especially density, I wondered if this fine-grained fabric might safeguard urban dwellers against the spread of the virus instead of increasing their exposure to it. The Mini Block City offers a mixed-use program, including housing, workplaces, cafes, convenience stores or small supermarkets, exercise clubs, and essential medical services. The project also includes beyond-everyday facilities, such as a cinema, dance hall, and other cultural amenities.

When a pandemic hits a city, the contagion can be contained within a limited area of one or several self-sufficient blocks, reducing the need to lock down an entire city while keeping the life inside and outside of the infected blocks as normal as possible. This idea invites greater specificity in development, beginning with the dimensions of a block. For example, 131 by 131 feet (40 by 40 meters) in Jiading might be too small to accommodate many uses within each block, but 164 x 164 feet (50 x 50 meters) could be the departure point since that is the size of blocks in many ancient cities worldwide.[20] Also, a mini block can't be designed as a unique piece of architecture. Instead, it must always be considered in the context of the larger neighborhood and nearby blocks. For example, a cluster of blocks can offer complementary commercial and cultural programs.

What is truly at stake here is the urban fabric. I want to remind everyone in our design community that we can't design a city for pandemics only. We must balance the quality of life for both sunny and rainy days. Urban life is communal, social, civic, and diverse. Nobody is willing to give it all up. We must design a city that is resilient—that is our way to fight back. After all, wanting to walk down the street to get a coffee with a friend is simply human nature.

Yung Ho Chang is the founding principal of Atelier FCJZ and a professor of the practice in the Department of Architecture at the Massachusetts Institute of Technology.

Atelier FCJZ, aerial view of an industrial park in Shanghai's Jiading district, 2020 / Tian Fangfang

The Pandemic Space
Theo Deutinger

**A detailed visual analysis of public
health distancing protocols reveals
the significant spatial influence of
COVID-19.**

—

Since the coronavirus pandemic first
appeared, our comprehension of space
has changed. We now have increased
distances, diminished densities, and
altered greeting habits. We did not fore-
see this transformation; instead, the
development of a new paradigm took us
by surprise. The recalculation of spatial
logics to protect the public against the
spread of COVID-19 came with shocking
speed. When the first wave of the pandemic swept through cities worldwide in
spring 2020, political leaders established
new distancing and behavioral protocols.
These decrees were primarily verbal,
not visual; therefore, the physical impact
was not immediately predictable.

A group of students from the University of Kassel and I analyzed, quantified,
and illustrated the new protocols to gain a
better understanding of their influence on
human activity and the built environment.
By translating these verbal designs into
actual plans, we revealed clear implications for architecture and urban design.
We called this new reality the Pandemic
Space. The City of Kassel functioned as
an initial case study for our analysis, and
we expanded our study to include many
international examples to reveal geo-
graphical similarities and differences in
approach. In our book *The Pandemic Space*,
we organized the content into seven chapters, which begins with specific programs
and eventually address the public domain:
the pandemic block, the pandemic
apartment, the pandemic city, pandemic
perfection in public parks, the pandemic

supplier, the pandemic culture, and the
pandemic protest.[21]

This project revealed both expected
and unexpected consequences of our
new spatial reality. As we anticipated,
person-to-person encounters are now
carefully negotiated, limiting permissible
room occupancies and encouraging contactless deliveries, for example. However,
when we mapped out different configurations of dwellings and occupants, the
reduction in usable living space for individuals was striking—particularly when
a family member must self-isolate. The
implications of social-distancing requirements on the public domain were also
notable, influencing pedestrian circulation, transportation infrastructure,
commercial activity, and dining. One
of the most intriguing studies concerned
the new protocols' effects on the path
dynamics of individuals and groups
moving through public parks.

This thorough spatial study inspired
us to wonder how long the Pandemic
Space will continue and in what forms.
How much plexiglass will remain in place,
continuing to barricade occupied areas?
How long will stickers last on benches,
identifying where not to sit? The answers
are difficult to predict in this rapidly evolving crisis. If COVID-19 weakens from a
pandemic to an endemic state, our work
will become part of the historical record.
If not, our book could become the user's
guide for combating ongoing outbreaks.
Regardless, this endeavor reveals the
importance of understanding the physical
implications of verbal decrees on architecture, cities, and people.

*Theo Deutinger is an architect, a writer,
and the founder of The Department (TD).*

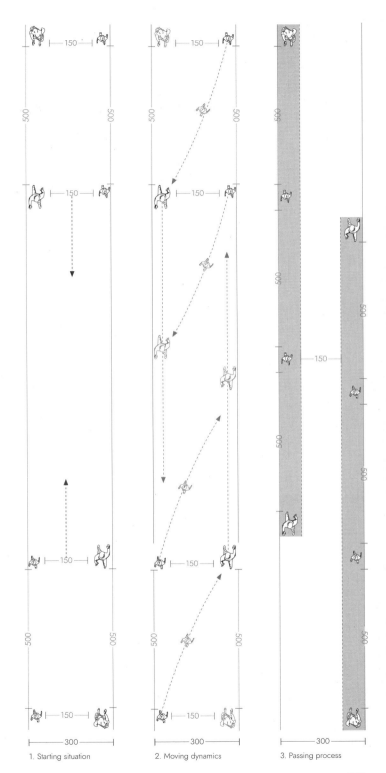

Theo Deutinger, drawing from *The Pandemic Space*, showing an encounter between two four-membered walking families, 2020 / Julia Rocho and Daniel Paul

1. Starting situation

2. Moving dynamics

3. Passing process

Covid Confessionals
Rachel Dickey and Noushin Radnia

Interactive public installations can improve the mental health of communities experiencing pandemic-related stress.

———

Covid Confessionals is a temporary public installation built as a rapid response to the COVID-19 pandemic. The project provides a place for interaction during a time of distressing social isolation with a series of occupiable "urban face shields." The installation employs the Center for Disease Control's six-foot social-distancing recommendation to avoid virus transmission as the modular basis of its design.

Unlike the clear plastic makeshift shields that appeared at grocery store checkout counters and other places of business to partition people, the walls of Covid Confessionals produce colorful caustic light patterns, resulting from the combined qualities of materiality and surface curvature. Made of flexible plastic and color-changing dichroic film, the partitions extrude upward from a grid of interconnected circles, each with a six-foot radius, providing transparent protective barriers between people. The iridescent, spectrum-shifting material appears different from all sides, providing an analog color-distortion filter through which to view oneself, each other, and the city.

The six-foot-interval spacing defines the location for curving barrier walls and provides the basis for the gridded structure, the placement of vibration-activated lights, and a demarcated ground mural. Triangulating lines from the connected circular-grid centers define the location of the prefabricated frame that supports the suspended walls. Additionally, a network of grid lines and touch-responsive light pads are located on the ground between the shields. These design elements demarcate zones for safely distanced interaction and play. Like disaster-relief shelters, the installation appropriates rapid-response construction strategies using off-the-shelf and prefabricated assemblies, including rigid metal conduit pipes, conduit connectors, and concrete deck blocks for the supporting structure.

Covid Confessionals provides a community space for in-person exchange in a time of emergency. The design suggests that considerations of health in architecture should extend beyond human physiology to include psychological implications. Rather than subverting mental-health issues, the installation manifests distancing measures architecturally and transforms social isolation into a matter of public importance. While the project does not suggest that architecture can solve the problem of social isolation, it responds to it, providing an alternative place for social exchange and playful interactions and reminding us of our capacity for resilience.

Rachel Dickey is an assistant professor in the School of Architecture at the University of North Carolina at Charlotte.

Noushin Radnia is an architectural research specialist with C Design and an adjunct instructor in the School of Architecture at the University of North Carolina at Charlotte.

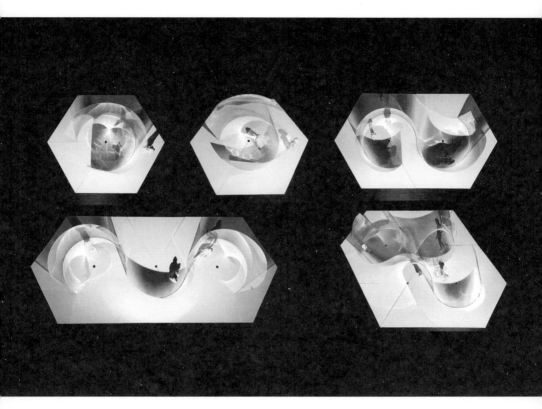

Studio Dickey, Covid Confessional models, 2021 / Studio Dickey

Prioritize Cycling Infrastructure

Jared Green

Improve resilience through safe and accessible bike lanes.

—

The SARS-CoV-2 virus changed many of our daily routines, including how we get around. During the worst of the pandemic, public-transit access was restricted in many communities or widely perceived as risky, causing bus and subway ridership to plummet. Many of those still riding buses and subways during lockdown were essential workers, who, perhaps, had no other choice because they couldn't afford or didn't have regular access to a car.

But the communities that had designed safe, protected bike lanes offered another option—one that helped drive urban-cycling rates to record highs, increased community health and resilience, and offered a sense of freedom during the height of pandemic fear.

During the lockdown in Washington, DC, my bike was my primary way of getting around the empty city. But as the police dealt with a range of other pressing problems, there was also a noticeable increase in dangerous driving, with drivers ignoring red lights or speeding down neighborhood streets. If we face another pandemic that seriously affects government services, it is, unfortunately, not hard to imagine streets feeling less safe for cyclists and pedestrians again.

I found myself relying on the district's protected bike lanes, which separate cyclists from vehicles through simple plastic bollards, curbs, paint, and parking spaces. They helped provide some sense of security amid the peak of the pandemic uncertainty. Numerous research studies have found that protected bike lanes not only make cyclists safer but also feel safer and are, therefore, the single-most important way to increase bike use among men and women, younger and older riders of all incomes and races. This phenomenon was true before the pandemic but became even more real during it.

Many communities that saw a temporary jump in cycling during the pandemic have seen an unfortunate return to the prepandemic status quo because this essential infrastructure wasn't in place. While pop-up bicycle lanes and "slow" or "open" streets have been valuable because they changed perceptions about what our shared roadways can become, more car-centric streets need to be permanently transformed into green, complete streets.

As cities reimagine their streets two years after the start of the pandemic, the most important step policymakers can take is to invest in planning and designing comprehensive and equitable networks of protected bike lanes that extend into historically marginalized and underserved communities and enable low-income residents to more easily bike to and from home, school, and work.

In cities that understand the many benefits of this infrastructure, landscape architects, planners, and engineers have already been connecting and upgrading bike lanes through a careful analysis of equity and use patterns and needs. They are also designing even better bicycle infrastructure—incorporating green infrastructure that safely separates bike, pedestrian, and vehicle uses and helps reduce flooding, urban temperatures, and air pollution. Of course, any infrastructure that increases bike rides as a percentage of total trips reduces greenhouse gas emissions from transportation, which account for 30 percent of total US emissions.

A protected bicycle lane in Sderot Chen, Tel Aviv-Yafo, Israel / Yoav Aziz

An equitable network of safe, protected bike lanes is one of the single best ways we can future-proof our cities and communities against an evolving SARS-CoV-2 virus and future pandemics and improve community health and well-being over the long term.

Jared Green is editor of **THE DIRT**, *the blog of the American Society of Landscape Architects. He authored* **Good Energy: Renewable Power and the Design of Everyday Life** *(2021) and edited* **Designed for the Future: 80 Practical Ideas for a Sustainable World** *(2015).*

Architectural Epidemiology

Adele Houghton and Carlos Castillo-Salgado

The pandemic has shown that design teams and public health experts must work together to consider the environmental health effects that extend beyond a project's site.

—

When the members of an architectural design team sit down to brainstorm a new project, they probably do not draw a bubble to separate the site from its surroundings. That kind of image is reserved for utopian (and dystopian) theorists like Claude Nicolas Ledoux and Étienne-Louis Boullée in eighteenth-century France, Superstudio in 1960s Italy, and the Biospherians in 1980s Arizona. But the reality is that real estate capital, building codes, and CAD software all orient architects to focus inside the property lines—often at the expense of the surrounding neighborhood.[22]

Society's initial response to the COVID-19 pandemic further reinforced the bubble metaphor. Healthcare providers encouraged us to create social "bubbles" to manage the spread.[23] The CDC released a COVID-19-prevention infographic with bubbles surrounding people walking down the street, children at school, and even entire homes.[24] Unfortunately, bubbles don't work. Every time members of a pandemic bubble interact with someone from outside, they risk introducing the virus into that safe space.[25] Similarly, if a school is located next to a freeway, some level of traffic-related air pollution will penetrate its air space, regardless of the number of structural and vegetative barriers erected to keep it out.[26]

Land use, building design, and facilities operations all play a role in a successfully layered public health response. Part of the response falls comfortably within the design bubble of standard practice: improved indoor air filtration, increased outdoor air-ventilation rates, enhanced cleaning protocols, and the like.[27] But that approach overlooks the role that land use and planning have played in creating the physical conditions for economic and health disparities in the US—disparities that the pandemic has emphasized.[28]

We propose a new transdisciplinary field called architectural epidemiology, which reorients design to place buildings in their social, ecological, and cultural contexts. From this perspective, the property line is not a barrier. It is a place of exchange between the site and the surrounding neighborhood. And it motivates the design team to coordinate with nearby properties in service of a larger goal, such as reducing the risk that children in the area will be exposed to traffic-related air pollution.

If there is one thing we have learned over the past few years, it is that no one is self-sufficient. At its best, architectural design catalyzes health, wellness, and community cohesion. The pandemic has taught us that the best way to realize that goal is to burst the property-line bubble.

Adele Houghton is an architect, a public health professional, and the coauthor of **Architectural Epidemiology** *(2023).*

Carlos Castillo-Salgado is a professor of epidemiology and the director of the Global Public Health Observatory at the Bloomberg School of Public Health, Johns Hopkins University, and the coauthor of **Architectural Epidemiology** *(2023).*

**Architectural Epidemiology redefines the property line as a place
of exchange rather than a barrier.** / Valeria Fursa

Picnic Right

Kaori Ito

Members of the Tokyo Picnic Club believe the pandemic experience will improve attitudes toward public space.
—

The Tokyo Picnic Club (TPC) was founded in Tokyo in 2002 to commemorate the two hundredth anniversary of the original Pic Nic Club in London.[29] Many of the members of TPC are creative professionals, including architects, urbanists, graphic designers, illustrators, gastronomists, landscape architects, and editors. Learning from the history of picnics, we explore the possibilities of the contemporary urban picnic. We also claim a "picnic right," promoting the use of urban public spaces.

In practice, we make a temporary picnic field appear in an urban public space, invite people to the picnic, and encourage them to rediscover local places and local foods. In addition, we host picnic competitions during which participants are evaluated on their food, picnic gear, and sociality to motivate people to demonstrate their creativity in daily life. We also collaborate with local industries to design original picnic foods and goods and plan picnic events. One of our major projects is Picnopolis, a large gathering that premiered in Newcastle/Gateshead, UK, in 2008 and has since taken place in Yokohama (2009), Singapore (2010), Osaka (2011), London (2012), and Fukuoka (2013).

When we started TPC, most people perceived the picnic as a childish pursuit irrelevant to urban space. Specialists were cynical about our activities as public space was largely dismissed in Japan at that time. However, the debate over public space has increased dramatically in the ensuing decades. The Japanese Ministry of Land, Infrastructure, Transport, and Tourism has deregulated the use of streets, riversides, and parks. Young architects, place makers, consultants, and journalists are involved in public-space projects, such as open cafes, parklets, and turfing. *Walkable* is now a buzzword in Japanese urban planning. However, while public space is attracting more attention than before, it tends to be dominated by marketing and fashion-based events.

The COVID-19 pandemic occurred just when public space was gaining increased attention in Japan. Since then, people have started preferring open-air places rather than closed facilities. Restaurants can sell to-go meals or put tables on the streets as an emergency response, and people spend more time in their neighborhood, discovering their local environment. Based on these changes, we ask, "Can the experience of the pandemic change consumeristic attitudes toward public space?"

Historically, Japanese people have excelled in cherishing outdoor spaces. They enjoyed the charms of each season, such as cherry-blossom viewing in the spring, relishing evening breezes in the summer, and moon-viewing or foliage-viewing in the fall. On such occasions, they wrote *waka* poems about seasonal scenes, enjoyed music and dance, and consumed tea, rice wine, or seasonal sweets. Today, we can once more cultivate a culture of everyday life in outdoor public spaces—a safer environment from a public health standpoint—transforming it into a place for contemporary creation and expression. A picnic is one of the first steps to make one's daily life more creative, enjoyable, and beautiful. We hope the experience of the pandemic gives people a chance to start their own picnic tradition.

Picnics during the pandemic in Marunouchi Street Park, Tokyo / Tokyo Picnic Club

*Kaori Ito is a professor of urban design
in the Department of Architecture at the
Tokyo University of Science.*

Curbside Table

Sheila Kennedy

The design of a simple piece of furniture can facilitate human connections during a challenging time.

———

In spring 2020, no one could fathom the magnitude and ongoing impacts of education, life events, and businesses being conducted primarily or partly online and the isolation of many people without reliable online access at home. In the context of the shelter-at-home mandate, business and school shutdowns, and the retreat (for some) online, people lost daily contact with ordinary physical things that enabled the construction of a common world. As Hannah Arendt argues in *The Human Condition*: "To live together in the world means essentially that a world of things is between those who have it in common, as a table is located between those who sit around it; the world, like every in-between, relates and separates [humans] at the same time."[30]

Our urban life together, no matter who we are, is built upon a world of things; the table that Arendt references is a microcosm of a larger social order—a support that itself takes shape around an array of ordinary material artifacts.[31] "The common world gathers us together and yet prevents our falling over each other, so to speak," Arendt writes, describing the image of a shared table that is present giving order to the people around it, only to disappear suddenly.[32]

A side table occupies a specific place and role in traditional interiors. It is a go-between, a mediator between people, spaces, and other pieces of furniture. The Curbside Table we designed is a piece of urban furniture that supports an emerging infrastructure of public care in the time of COVID-19. The design meets the need for social distancing as a primary way of avoiding illness without supporting the technological apparatus of dimensioned body allocation, barrier construction, and the enforced physical separation of people. The table establishes a shared threshold between an exterior urban world and the interior of a business struggling to operate while being closed to the public. Located at the curbside, it serves small businesses as a portable, contactless transfer station where goods and essential items are exchanged within easy reach. Drawing on traditions of street markets, threshold stands, and microstorefronts, the table offers a simple, forward-looking vision for new and needed collective urban practices of caring and sharing.

The rapid deployability of the Curbside Table brought it into the realm of political protests occurring in May 2020 after the murder of George Floyd. In this societal context of protest, the table became useful for civilian movements, including BLM, during which organizers could operate out of the back of a car and set up a Curbside Table to distribute masks, information, and petitions. A group of BLM organizers, whom we never met, anonymously promoted the Curbside Table in the local media.[33]

As we continue to inhabit this devastating health crisis, our team chooses to focus on design as a form of agency that brings people together to support public speech, discourse, and the essential diversity of urban public life. As a form of counterintelligence, the Curbside Table is a design and a set of social actions that offer new formats for urban care in the face of increasing division, isolation, and inequity in our cities.

KVA MATx, Curbside Table, Orinoco, Cambridge, Massachusetts, 2020 / KVA MATx

above: **KVA MATx, Curbside Tables, Elmendorf Baking Supplies & Cafe, Cambridge, Massachusetts, 2020** / KVA MATx
below: **KVA MATx, Curbside Table production drawing, 2020** / KVA MATx

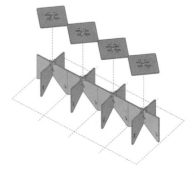

Sheila Kennedy is a principal of Kennedy & Violich Architecture and a professor of architecture at the Massachusetts Institute of Technology.

Natural Healing

Erica Timko Olson

***Shinrin-yoku*, or "forest-bathing," facilitates the body's innate restorative capacity.**

—

When you're sick, a hospital is not the place where you're going to get well. The aim of medicine is to put the body in the best condition to heal, but medicine doesn't perform the healing. The body heals itself. Antibiotics and chemotherapy assist with this goal, but they don't do the work of restoration. The body must do this work, and this process should occur within a healthy, natural environment.

I grew up on a farm in southwest Minnesota. When my father passed away ten years ago, I returned to the family farm. I didn't realize how little we had—and at the same time, how much, surrounded by expansive gardens. I remembered a conversation I had with my father before he died. I was living in Philadelphia at the time, surrounded by a big city lacking ample green space. I told him I felt out of sorts. "When was the last time you saw the horizon?" he asked.

My work focuses on the concept of spiritual resilience in connection with nature. For my PhD research, I examined the relationship between anxiety, resilience, and spirituality. Spirituality increases resilience, and resilience decreases anxiety, for example. I have analyzed the connections between mindfulness and *shinrin-yoku*. In one study, my coauthors and I assessed human neurobiological, neuroendocrine, and emotional responses to natural environments.[34] We found a measurable positive correlation between exposure to nature and psychological well-being. Therefore, we surmised that at-risk groups, such as those experiencing social isolation and depression due to the COVID-19 pandemic, would benefit significantly from the cost-effective, preventative modality of shinrin-yoku.

The disruption and uncertainty created by the coronavirus disease have led to much anxiety. But anxiety is not the biggest problem—isolation is. We need to focus on building communities that are surrounded by nature—living landscapes in which we can live and work together. Like the body, nature is always seeking homeostasis. Nature can give us purpose and reinforce our reciprocal relationship with it. As we invest in nature, nature invests in us. It's not about throwing a plant in someone's office or having a green wall. It's about the totality of experience—the flow of air and light, the interconnections between multiple living systems. Biophilia—the instinctive aim humans have to connect with nature—must be at the center of our built environment. By pursuing biophilic design strategies, we can create the best opportunity for people to heal physically, mentally, and spiritually.

Erica Timko Olson is a clinical assistant professor in the School of Nursing at the University of Minnesota.

Steven Kamenar, *Untitled* / Steven Kamenar

Flattening the Curve of Cities

Carlo Ratti

Strategies to mitigate the spread of pandemics can be adopted to optimize urban mobility.

—

The opening clip of the 1999 comedy *Office Space* takes an unflinching look at a traffic jam. Drivers inch forward in a pathetic dance of honking and changing lanes, exhausted and enraged by the daily gridlock of a California highway. Congestion is a necessary evil of human agglomeration and has characterized cities since antiquity. Yet today, it could be mitigated with the same strategy we adopted to fight a once-in-a-century pandemic: flattening the curve.

Before vaccines were widely rolled out, the flattening-the-curve mantra was our primary strategy to combat COVID-19. This approach aimed to spread contagion over time. Lockdowns, social distancing, and masks did not stop the virus, but they slowed it down so that our ventilators, beds, and healthcare workers would be less overwhelmed. Such a practice saved lives in the early days of the pandemic.

The same approach also has the potential to save our cities. Our urban infrastructure frequently suffers from high peaks of demand. Morning commuters jam our highways and lead to painful, congested standstills. At lunchtime, massive lines form. Finally, traveling back home at the end of the day pushes our mobility infrastructure (and our power grids) to the limit.

It might seem tempting to just widen our roads and augment power production. However, such an approach would result in an expensive, oversized infrastructure that goes unused for most of the day. A better option would be changing usage patterns and reducing peaks, thus making our cities more affordable and efficient.

Months into the pandemic, we were getting used to a more flexible living schedule. If we could start commuting on a staggered basis, it would not only reduce contagion risk but also have the added benefit of spreading out the times when people use the road. For example, if some of us attend a 9:00 p.m. meeting over Zoom from home and arrive at the office at noon, and others leave at 3:00 a.m. to wrap up the day online, rush hour would no longer be an issue.

More structured policies can also be put in place to ensure infrastructure usage spikes are further reduced. For example, Singapore's Electronic Road Pricing has succeeded for more than twenty years at reducing peak demand. A similar approach in the energy industry known as "peak-shaving" is extremely impactful for cost savings and the environment. As the IoT grows more sophisticated, we can improve these models with the power of digital sensing and individual incentives, perhaps traded via blockchain.[35]

That said, the system should be perfected so that it does not leave anyone behind. Congestion fees can encourage some people to change their habits. Still, many—warehouse employees, school custodians, or Uber drivers—do not have the flexibility to reschedule their lives or the liquidity to afford regressive tolls. Just as flattening the curve of the pandemic came with financial support for low-income groups who could not work and study remotely, flattening the curve of urban-infrastructure usage must foreground questions of equity.

The opening scene of *Office Space* is a reminder that daily traffic jams are

CRA-Carlo Ratti Associati, "New Deal Paris," Forum Métropolitain du Grand Paris, France, 2019 / CRA-Carlo Ratti Associati

absurd, and our rapid societal change is a reminder that they may not be necessary. Flattening the curve was a painful response to a health crisis to save our lives, but in the future, it might help save our cities.

Carlo Ratti is the founding partner of CRA-Carlo Ratti Associati and a professor in the Department of Urban Studies and Planning at the Massachusetts Institute of Technology.

Nearby Nature
Naomi A. Sachs

The emergence of the coronavirus pandemic was the moment the outdoors became essential.

—

The coronavirus pandemic rapidly changed how people interacted with the outdoor and natural world. As everyone grappled with uncertainty, one fact was clear early on: this deadly airborne disease was more transmissible indoors than out. Suddenly, the outdoors was safer, and "getting a breath of fresh air" took on new meaning.

During the first quarantine lockdowns in the spring of 2020, in all but a few countries, citizens were told to stay home but were encouraged—or at least allowed—to go outside for a few minutes a day. For the first time, many people noticed "nearby nature"—flora and fauna just beyond their windows. Nature felt like the only normal thing. Spring bulbs emerging from frozen soil were a promise of renewal. Trees budding, then blooming, then leafing were symbols of life and its beautiful cycle. People fortunate to have a yard began gardening or changed their gardening habits. Instagram pulsed with #Covidgardening posts of hastily constructed gardens and the resulting beautiful, nourishing produce enjoyed without terrifying trips to the grocery store.

With most indoor spaces closed, the outdoors became our gym, office, classroom, and living room. Dyed-in-the-wool nature lovers complained that their favorite quiet outdoor spaces were now overrun with people. Parks in Singapore employed robotic dogs to enforce social distancing; parks in New York City painted circles on lawns, each circle's edge six feet apart from the next.

At the same time that natural areas were flooded with new visitors, some parks became overflow treatment spaces for healthcare facilities. For example, Mount Sinai Health System's sixty-eight-bed-tent emergency field hospital in Central Park looked like a scene from the Crimean War. Images of the field hospital were particularly poignant to those who knew that Frederick Law Olmsted, codesigner of Central Park, served as executive secretary of the United States Sanitary Commission (a precursor to the Red Cross) before devoting himself to landscape architecture.[36] To Olmsted, parks were "the lungs of the city," essential and democratic spaces where all people could gather.

Mount Sinai also set up Recharge Rooms for stressed healthcare workers at several of its hospitals. The Recharge Room at Beth Israel was a former triage tent in the parking lot. Nature sounds and videos, live plants, and soft lighting gave care providers a feeling of immersion in nature. Hospital healing gardens saw a surge in usage by care providers. One landscape architect shared the following with me: "The…gardens have experienced a three to four times increase.…The quantity of people is near the amount that shows up when there is an event. Now is an open door to educate about the virtues of nature in our lives." [37]

It is too soon to tell what positive effects such a sudden and dramatic shift toward the outdoors will have long-term. People like me who advocate for safe, equitable access to nature in healthcare and beyond hope that the change will be permanent and long-lasting, that like new growth emerging from scorched

The emphasis on nearby nature is seen in projects like Jean Nouvel's Cartier Foundation for Contemporary Art, Paris, France, 1994 / Blaine Brownell

earth after a fire, people's newfound love of nature will take root and nurture us for generations to come.

Naomi A. Sachs is an assistant professor in the Department of Plant Science and Landscape Architecture at the University of Maryland and the founding director of the Therapeutic Landscapes Network.

Samaritan Services
Ulysses Sean Vance

Altruistic healthcare beyond hospital walls provides essential support for underserved populations.

—

Hospital space is shrinking. According to the COVID-19 Hospitalization Tracking Project, the most extreme urban and rural hospitals reported overcrowded ICU beds upward of 75 percent capacity in 2020 and again in 2022. With the continued surge in medical care and, in particular, the long-term intubation of patients, space for procedure comes at a premium. Concurrently, per the American Hospital Association, the expense per capita in the hospital is approximately $4,500 per patient, and considering that in these conditions patients are primarily confined to a bed in a shared environment, the cost for recovery in these spaces is significant. This exponential price increase drives patient facilities to decrease space devoted to long-term care, reducing patient privacy to facilitate overcrowding. Cases like these are happening worldwide as patients, turned away from medical care if their condition is not life-threatening, have to find solace in waiting for their conditions to worsen. By comparing the number of instances per week of Covid against the number of available beds, we can evaluate the urgency facilities encounter when treating patients suffering from COVID-19 while working to maintain other in-patient services. Therefore, it is logical to conceive that the continued increase in challenges associated with finding medical service would continue to alienate those for whom medical fears push them further away from care.

Counter to the apparent demise in the previous narrative, philanthropic groups, such as the Black Doctors Consortium, indiscriminately provide care through both medical and nonmedical engagements.[38] Moreover, the actions of these individual citizens and doctors are expanding healthcare's engagement to underserved persons with minimal support, often at their own expense. Although they are also constantly working in underutilized spaces and directly distributing services from mobile units, their efforts have improved the condition of services currently in practice. Markedly, a select few have begun to regularize their services, working in the liminal spaces of neighborhoods, often between activities of their professional practices and bracketed by a gamut of other public health crises of food insecurity, social isolation, and trauma-related violence.

Where are patients going when there is no longer ample space in medical facilities and the mobile units are not in their vicinity? Notably, the places proven to be highly effective in administering health services are the nonmedical facilities where persons would typically not seek medical attention. Mainly, practices worldwide show they tend to seek assistance in the most familiar places, the barbershop, the bodega, or the retail pharmacy, when available. Like the practice of medical triage in hospitals, these nonmedical spaces attend to demand based on the severity of the need. Knowing that the current overcrowding crisis in healthcare facilities will persist, it is alarming that the situations in urban and rural regions have continued to escalate to these current conditions. Despite this reality, many of these Samaritan services will continue to offer support where they can, even though they are not readily or easily capable of maintaining the service models beyond the immediate future.

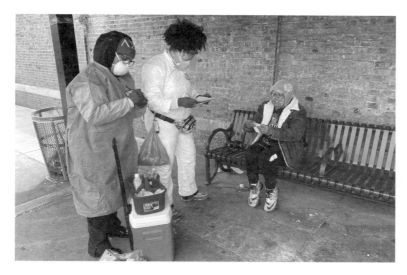

Healthcare professionals offering street-side medical consultations, Philadelphia, Pennsylvania, 2020 / Marshall Mitchell

Dr. Ala Stanford, founder of the Black Doctor's Consortium, consulting with a patient in Philadelphia, Pennsylvania, 2020 / Marshall Mitchell

Ulysses Sean Vance is an associate professor of architecture in the Tyler School of Art and Architecture at Temple University.

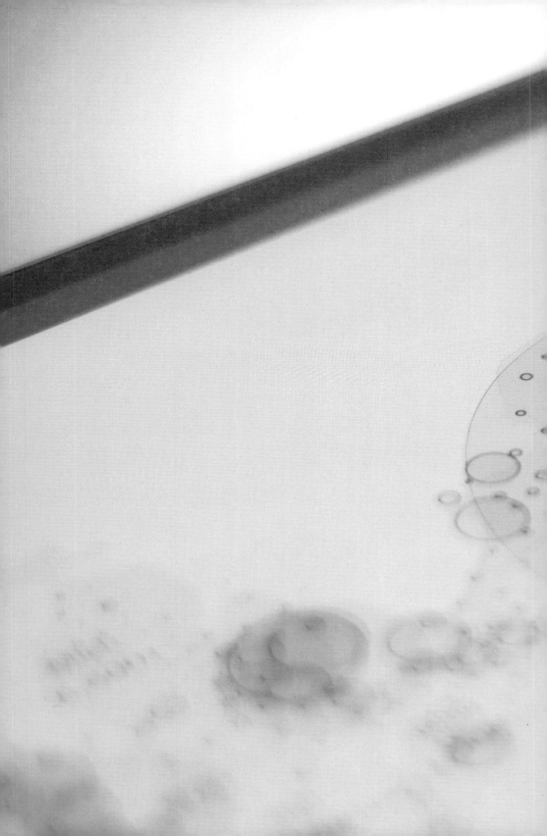

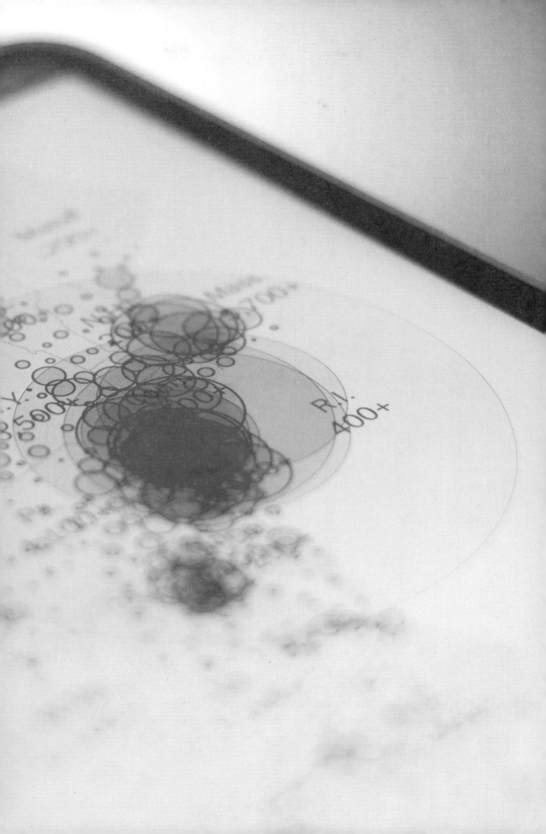

Acknowledgments

This project emerged from a collection of online articles I wrote about the COVID-19 pandemic for *Architect* magazine beginning in spring 2020. I have been fortunate to serve as a regular contributing editor to *Architect* since 2011, and this platform has enabled me to focus on significant matters, like the coronavirus pandemic, as events unfold. I am deeply grateful to *Architect* colleagues Ned Cramer, Wanda Lau, Katie Gerfen, Katherine Keane, Eric Wills, and Alexandra Cipolle of Hanley Wood Business Media and Zonda Media for their support of this work.

The themes and questions raised by these articles found their way into lectures I gave to academic and professional audiences, including the McCoy Center for Ethics in Society at Stanford University, the Modern Literature and Culture Research Center at Ryerson University, the School of Architecture at the University of North Carolina at Charlotte, the International Interior Design Association, and the American Institute of Architects' Aspire South Atlantic Region and Alabama, Florida, and Oklahoma chapters. I am grateful to these institutions and organizations for the opportunities to share—and receive feedback on—these topics.

I was invited to direct the University of North Carolina at Charlotte School of Architecture in early 2020, on the eve of the pandemic, and experienced a cross-country move during that first, bizarre COVID-19 summer. Despite the uncertainties of making a transition under such circumstances, I was warmly welcomed by this vibrant and exceptional community of scholars, practitioners, and educators. I want to thank Brook Muller, Dean of the College of Arts + Architecture, for extending the invitation to join UNC Charlotte. I would also like to thank my School of Architecture faculty, staff, and students—as well as my new colleagues in the college and university—for their support. I am especially grateful to Sarah Auger, my research assistant, for her help with this effort. Fortuitously, many UNC Charlotte faculty are pursuing meaningful research related to the themes in this book, and I am appreciative of their contributions included here.

I would also like to thank all other contributors for committing valuable time and energy to this book. Your work inspires me and offers much-needed visions for a postpandemic world.

I am indebted to Princeton Architectural Press executive editor Jennifer Thompson for believing in this project and for being my close collaborator and sounding board throughout its development and execution. We have worked together for a rewarding seventeen years now. Here's to the next seventeen! It has also been a thrill to work with editor Linda Lee and designer Paul Wagner again. The band reunited for this project! I couldn't imagine a better team.

Finally, I am most grateful to my wife, Heather, and sons, Blaine and Davis, for their tireless support and encouragement.

Notes

Introduction

1. Klepeis et al., "The National Human Activity Pattern Survey (NHAPS): A Resource for Assessing Exposure to Environmental Pollutants," *Journal of Exposure Analysis and Environmental Epidemiology* 11 (July 26, 2001): 231–52, https://www.nature.com/articles/7500165.pdf.

2. Hui-Yi Yeh, Kou-Huang Chen, and Kow-Tong Chen, "Environmental Determinants of Infectious Disease Transmission: A Focus on One Health Concept," *International Journal of Environmental Research and Public Health* 15 (June 6, 2018), https://www.ncbi.nlm.nih.gov/pmc/articles/PMC6025375/.

3. Shuang Ma, Shuangjin Li, and Junyi Zhang, "Diverse and Nonlinear Influences of Built Environment actors on COVID-19 Spread Across Townships in China at Its Initial Stage," *Scientific Reports* 11 (June 14, 2021), https://www.nature.com/articles/s41598-021-91849-1.

4. Bo Li, You Peng, He He, Mingshu Wang, and Tao Feng, "Built Environment and Early Infection of COVID-19 in Urban Districts: A Case Study of Huangzhou," *Sustainable Cities and Society* 66 (December 26, 2020), https://www.ncbi.nlm.nih.gov/pmc/articles/PMC7836794/.

5. Chao Liu, Zerun Liu, and ChengHe Guan, "The Impacts of the Built Environment on the Incidence Rate of COVID-19: A Case Study of King County, Washington," *Sustainable Cities and Society* 74 (July 10, 2021), https://www.ncbi.nlm.nih.gov/pmc/articles/PMC8271037/.

6. Michael Gochfeld and Bernard D. Goldstein, "Lessons in Environmental Health in the Twentieth Century," *Annual Review of Public Health* 20 (May 1999), https://www.annualreviews.org/doi/10.1146/annurev.publhealth.20.1.35.

7. Ibid.

8. Ibid.

9. Beatriz Colomina, *X-Ray Architecture* (Zurich, Switzerland: Lars Müller Publishers, 2019), 10.

10. *Merriam Webster,* s.v. "sanitize," accessed April 25, 2022,https://www.merriam-webster.com/dictionary/sanitize.

11. John Vidal, "Destruction of Habitat and Loss of Biodiversity Are Creating the Perfect Conditions for Diseases Like COVID-19 to Emerge," *Ensia,* March 17, 2020, https://ensia.com/features/COVID-19-coronavirus-biodiversity-planetary-health-zoonoses/.

12. Ibid.

13. Edwin Choi and Juhan Sonin, "Determinants of Health," *GoInvo,* accessed April 25, 2022, https://www.goinvo.com/vision/determinants-of-health/.

14. Ibid.

15. Jonathan Leider, Christine Plepys, and Brian Castrucci, "Trends in the Conferral of Graduate Public Health Degrees: A Triangulated Approach," *Public Health Reports* 133 (September 19, 2018), https://journals.sagepub.com/doi/full/10.1177/0033354918791542.

16. Steven H. Woolf and Laudan Aron, eds., *U.S. Health in International Perspective: Shorter Lives, Poorer Health* (Washington, DC: National Academies Press, 2013), 192, https://www.ncbi.nlm.nih.gov/books/NBK154491/.

17. Ibid.

18. Paula Braveman and Laura Gottlieb, "The Social Determinants of Health: It's Time to Consider the Causes of the Causes," *Public Health Reports* 129 (Jan–Feb 2014), https://www.ncbi.nlm.nih.gov/pmc/articles/PMC3863696/.

19. See definition of "Letters" under "Types of Articles," *ACSA Energy Letters,* accessed April 25, 2022, https://pubs.acs.org/page/aelccp/about.html.

20. *Merriam Webster,* s.v. "immunize," accessed April 25, 2022, https://www.merriam-webster.com/dictionary/immunize.

Chapter One

1. Jocelyne Piret and Guy Bolvin, "Pandemics Throughout History," *Frontiers in Microbiology* 11 (January 15, 2021): 2, https://www.frontiersin.org/articles/10.3389/fmicb.2020.631736/full.

2. Ibid, 1.

3. Dana Grennan, "What Is a Pandemic?" *Journal of American Medical Association* 321, no. 9 (March 6, 2019): 1, https://jamanetwork.com/journals/jama/fullarticle/2726986.

4. Peter Sands, "Why Aren't Diseases Like HIV and Malaria, Which Still Kill Millions of People a Year, Called Pandemics?" *Stat,* July 6, 2021, https://www.statnews.com/2021/07/06/why-arent-diseases-like-hiv-and-malaria-which-still-kill-millions-of-people-a-year-called-pandemics/.

5. Piret and Bolvin, "Pandemics Throughout History," 2.

6.Ananias Escalante, Denise Freeland, William Collins, and Altaf Lal, "The Evolution of Primate Malaria Parasites Based on the Gene Encoding Cytochrome b from the Linear Mitochondrial

Genome," *Proceedings of the National Academies of Sciences* 95 (July 7, 1998), https://www.pnas.org/content/95/14/8124.

7. Jacques Jouanna, "Cause and Crisis in Historians and Medical Writers of the Classical Period," in *Hippocrates in Context: Papers Read at the XIth International Hippocrates Colloquium*, ed. P. J. van der Eijk (Newcastle Upon Tyne, UK: University of Newcastle upon Tyne, August 2002): 17.

8. Eugenia Tognotti, "Lessons from the History of Quarantine, from Plague to Influenza A," *Emerging Infectious Diseases* 19, no. 2 (February 2013): 255, https://www.ncbi.nlm.nih.gov/pmc/articles/PMC3559034/.

9. Theodore H. Tulchinsky, "John Snow, Cholera, the Broad Street Pump; Waterborne Diseases Then and Now," *Case Studies in Public Health* (March 30, 2018): 77, https://www.ncbi.nlm.nih.gov/pmc/articles/PMC7150208/.

10. Margaret Campbell, "What Tuberculosis did for Modernism: The Influence of a Curative Environment on Modernist Design and Architecture," *Medical History* (October 1, 2005), https://www.ncbi.nlm.nih.gov/pmc/articles/PMC1251640/.

11. Benjamin Ward Richardson, "Health in the Home," in *Our Homes and How to Make them Healthy*, ed. Shirley Forster Murphy (London: Cassell & Company, 1883), 5.

12. Robert Boyle first coined the term "factitious airs" upon discovering hydrogen in 1671 when he diluted sulfuric acid and iron.

13. Dorothy A. Stansfield and Ronald G. Stansfield, "Dr. Thomas Beddoes and James Watt: Preparatory Work 1794–1796 for the Bristol Pneumatic Institute," *Medical History* 30 (1986), 276–302, 296.

14. Stansfield and Stansfield, 290.

15. Michelle Murphy, *Sick Building Syndrome and the Problem of Uncertainty* (Durham, North Carolina: Duke University Press, 2006).

16. Marsha Coleman-Adebayo, *No Fear: A Whistleblower's Triumph Over Corruption and Retaliation at the EPA* (Chicago: Lawrence Hill Books, 2011).

17. "Stress, the 'Health Epidemic of the 21st Century,'" *HCA Healthcare Today*, April 30, 2019, https://hcahealthcaretoday.com/2019/04/30/stress-the-health-epidemic-of-the-21st-century/.

18. Herman Melville, *Bartleby the Scrivener: A Story of Wall Street* (New York: Harper Collins, reprinted 2009), 37.

19. Parts of this text and the collage drawing were initially created as part of a 2020 Instagram series called #UrbanismBeyondCorona edited/hosted by Urban Works Agency (which the author codirects) and the Experimental History Project at the California College of the Arts Architecture Division.

20. Andrea Bagnato, "Staying at Home," *e-flux*, May 2020, https://www.e-flux.com/architecture/at-the-border/329404/staying-at-home/.

21. Mitch McEwen, "What Does Trayvon's Shooting Mean for Architects and Urbanists?" *Huffington Post*, May 30, 2012, https://www.huffpost.com/entry/what-does-sanford-florida_b_1392677.

22. Emily Brink and William Taylor, "Architecture and Crowd-Less Streets: Urban and Environmental Order, Absence, and Risk in Pierre Patte's Profil d'une rue (1769)," Architectural Theory Review 23, no. 2 (2019): 1–17. See also Andrew J. Tallon, "The Portuguese Precedent for Pierre Patte's Street Section," Journal of the Society of Architectural Historians 63, no. 3 (2004): 370–77.

23. Matthew Gandy, *Concrete and Clay: Reworking Nature in New York City.* (Cambridge, MA: MIT Press, 2002).

24. Dolores Hayden, *The Grand Domestic Revolution: A History of Feminist Designs For American Homes, Neighborhoods, and Cities* (Cambridge, MA: MIT Press, 1981) and Anna Puigjaner, "Bringing the Kitchen Out of the House," e-flux, February 2019, https://www.e-flux.com/architecture/overgrowth/221624/bringing-the-kitchen-out-of-the-house/.

25. Le Corbusier, *Toward a New Architecture*, trans. Frederick Etchells (Mineola, New York: Dover Publications, 1986).

Chapter Two

1. "Indoor Air and Coronavirus (COVID-19)," *United States Environmental Protection Agency*, accessed April 25, 2022, https://www.epa.gov/coronavirus/indoor-air-and-coronavirus-covid-19.

2. Ibid.

3. Ashraf Mimi Elsaid, Hany Mohamed, Gamal Abdelaziz, and M. Salem Ahmede, "A Critical Review of Heating, Ventilation, and Air Conditioning (HVAC) Systems within the Context of a Global SARS-CoV-2 Epidemic," *Process Safety and Environmental Protection*, September 20, 2021, https://www.ncbi.nlm.nih.gov/pmc/articles/PMC8450051/.

4. Thom Dunn, "Can Air Conditioning Transmit the Coronavirus?" *New York Times*, July 13, 2020, https://www.nytimes.com/wirecutter/blog/air-conditioning-coronavirus/.

5. Himanshu Agarwal, "Why We Must Prioritize Sanitization of Indoor Air in the Wake of COVID-19," *Entrepreneur India*, July 2, 2020, https://www.entrepreneur.com/article/352740.

6. "Can an HVAC Duct Spread COVID-19 in Offices, Stores and Schools?" *Hartford Healthcare*, July 13, 2020, https://hartfordhealthcare.org/about-us/news-press/news-detail?articleid=27158&publicId=395.

7. "Air Cleaners, HVAC Filters, and Coronavirus (COVID-19)," *United States Environmental Protection Agency*, accessed April 25, 2022, https://www.epa.gov/coronavirus/air-cleaners-hvac-filters-and-coronavirus-COVID-19.

8. "Inefficient Air Conditioning Drives Global Warming, UN Report Finds," *EcoWatch*, July 21, 2020, https://www.ecowatch.com/air-conditioning-2646444619.html.

9. Günter Kampf, "Biocidal Agents Used for Disinfection Can Enhance Antibiotic Resistance in Gram-Negative Species," *Antibiotics*, December 14, 2018, https://www.ncbi.nlm.nih.gov/pmc/articles/PMC6316403/.

10. Dorit Aviv, Kian Wee Chen, Eric Teitelbaum, Denon Sheppard, Jovan Pantelic, Adam Rysanek, and Forrest Meggers, "A Fresh (Air) Look at Ventilation for COVID-19: Estimating the Global Energy Savings Potential of Coupling Natural Ventilation with Novel Radiant Cooling Strategies," *Applied Energy* 292 (March 22, 2021), https://www.ncbi.nlm.nih.gov/pmc/articles/PMC7983460/.

11. Sarah Boslaugh, "Sick Building Syndrome," *Encyclopedia Britannica*, April 5, 2021, https://www.britannica.com/science/sick-building-syndrome.

12. Ibid.

13. Sarah B. Henderson, Kathleen E. McLean, Michael Lee, and Tom Kosatsky, "Extreme Heat Events Are Public Health Emergencies," *BC Medical Journal* 63, no. 9 (November 2021), https://bcmj.org/bccdc/extreme-heat-events-are-public-health-emergencies; and Corina Stetiu, "Energy and Peak Power Savings Potential of Radiant Cooling Systems in U.S. Commercial Buildings," Energy and Buildings 30, no. 2 (June 1999), https://www.sciencedirect.com/science/article/pii/S0378778898000802.

14. Aviv, "A Fresh (Air) Look."

15. Helmut E. Feustel, Corina Stetiu, "Hydronic Radiant Cooling Preliminary Assessment," *Energy and Buildings* 22 (August 1, 1995), https://www.aivc.org/sites/default/files/airbase_9029.pdf.

16. Friedrich Kittler, *Gramophone, Film, Typewriter*, trans. Geoffrey Winthrop-Young, and Michael Wutz (Stanford, California: Stanford University Press: 1999), xxxix.

17. Richard J. de Dear and Gail S. Brager, "Toward an Adaptive Model of Thermal Comfort and Preference," *ASHRAE Transactions* 104, no. 1 (1998): 145–67.

18. Gail Brager, Sam Borgeson, and Soo Lee Yoon, *Summary Report: Control Strategies for Mixed-Mode Buildings* (Berkeley: Center for the Built Environment, University of California, 2007).

19. Andrew Cruse, "Improving the Weather: On Architectural Comforts and Climates," in *Examining the Environmental Impacts of Materials and Buildings*, ed. Blaine Brownell (Hershey, PA: IGI Global, 2020), 251–81.

20. Alison and Peter Smithson, *The Charged Void: Architecture* (New York: Monacelli, 2001), 552.

21. bell hooks, *Belonging: A Culture of Place* (New York: Routledge, 2009), 121.

22. Ibid.

23. Jane Jacobs, *The Death and Life of Great American Cities* (New York: Knopf Doubleday Publishing Group, 2016), 56.

24. Roger Ulrich, Robert Simons, Barbara Losito, Evelyn Fiorito, Mark Miles, and Michael Zelson, "Stress Recovery During Exposure to Natural and Urban Environments," *Journal of Environmental Psychology* 11, no. 3 (1991): 201–30, https://www.sciencedirect.com/science/article/pii/S0272494405801847; and Rachel Kaplan and Stephen Kaplan, *The Experience of Nature: A Psychological Perspective* (Cambridge, UK: Cambridge University Press, 1989).

25. Aaron Antonovsky, *Health, Stress and Coping* (San Francisco: Jossey-Bass Publishers, 1979).

26. "A Community of Care," *GBBN*, accessed April 25, 2022, https://www.gbbn.com/work/trihealth-harold-m-and-eugenia-s-thomas-comprehensive-care-center/.

27. Henry Dicks, "The Philosophy of Biomimicry," *Philosophy and Technology* 29 (2016), https://philpapers.org/rec/DICTPO-8.

28. Gail S. Brager and Richard J. de Dear, "Historical and Cultural Influences on Comfort Expectations," in *Buildings, Culture and Environment: Informing Local and Global Practices*, ed. Raymond J. Cole and Richard Lorch (John Wiley & Sons, 2008), 177–201; and Laura J. Martin et al., "Evolution of the Indoor Biome," *Trends in Ecology & Evolution* 30, no. 4 (April 1, 2015): 223–32, https://doi.org/10.1016/j.tree.2015.02.001.

29. Mary Douglas, *Purity and Danger: An Analysis of Concepts of Pollution and Taboo* (London: Routledge, 2002), https://doi.org/10.4324/9780203361832; and tephanie J. Dancer, "Infection Control in the Post-Antibiotic Era," *Healthcare Infection* 18, no. 2 (April 10, 2013): 51–60, https://doi.org/10.1071/HI12042.S
30. Nancy Tomes, *The Gospel of Germs: Men, Women, and the Microbe in American Life* (Cambridge, MA: Harvard University Press, 1998).
31. Ai Hisano, "Cellophane, the New Visuality, and the Creation of Self-Service Food Retailing," *SSRN Electronic Journal*, May 25, 2017, https://papers.ssrn.com/sol3/papers.cfm?abstract_id=2973544.
32. Tomes, *The Gospel of Germs*.
33. Werner Oechslin, "'Transparency': The Search for a Reliable Design Method in Accordance with the Principles of Modern Architecture," in *Transparency*, eds. Colin Rowe and Robert Slutzky (Basel: Birkhauser, 1997), 9–20.
34. David Yeomans, "The Pre-History of the Curtain Wall," *Construction History* 14 (1998): 59–82, https://www.jstor.org/stable/41601861.
35. David Harvey, "The Right to the City," *New Left Review* 53 (Sep/Oct 2008), https://newleftreview.org/issues/ii53/articles/david-harvey-the-right-to-the-city.

Chapter Three

1. "The CDC Prevention Strategy," *Centers for Disease Control and Prevention*, accessed April 25, 2022, https://ftp.cdc.gov/pub/infectious_diseases/emergplan/pdf/strategy.pdf.
2. Ibid., 15.
3. Gary Wolf, "Know Thyself: Tracking Every Facet of Life, from Sleep to Mood to Pain, 24/7/365," *Wired*, June 22, 2009, https://www.wired.com/2009/06/lbnp-knowthyself/.
4. Erik Jaspers and Eric Teicholz, "The Quantified Building," *International Facilities Management Journal* (March/April 2016): 40-45, http://fmj.ifma.org/publication/?m=30261&i=295044&p=40&ver=html5.
5. Ibid.
6. "Hierarchy of Controls," *Centers for Disease Control and Prevention*, accessed April 25, 2022, https://www.cdc.gov/niosh/topics/hierarchy/default.html.
7. "Implementing a Layered Approach to Address COVID-19 in Public Indoor Spaces," *United States Environmental Protection Agency*, accessed April 25, 2022, https://www.epa.gov/coronavirus/implementing-layered-approach-address-COVID-19-public-indoor-spaces.

8. "Guidance on Preparing Workplaces for COVID-19," *Occupational Safety and Health Administration* (2020 ok?), accessed April 25, 2022, https://www.osha.gov/sites/default/files/publications/OSHA3990.pdf.
9. Angela Eykelbosh, "A Rapid Review of the Use of Physical Barriers in Non-Clinical Settings and COVID-19 Transmission," *National Collaborating Center for Environmental Health*, November 17, 2021, https://ncceh.ca/documents/evidence-review/rapid-review-use-physical-barriers-non-clinical-settings-and-COVID-19.
10. Richard Gray, "Covid-19: How Long Does the Coronavirus Last on Surfaces?" *BBC*, March 17, 2020, https://www.bbc.com/future/article/20200317-covid-19-how-long-does-the-coronavirus-last-on-surfaces.
11. Stephen Ashkin, "Pros and Cons of Antimicrobial Surface Coatings," *Cleaning and Maintenance Management*, January 29, 2016, https://www.cmmonline.com/articles/pros-and-cons-of-antimicrobial-surface-coatings.
12. Wenwu Tang et al., "A Web-based Spatial Decision Support System of Wastewater Surveillance for COVID-19 Monitoring: A Case Study of a University Campus," *medRxiv*, January 1, 2022, https://www.medrxiv.org/content/10.1101/2021.12.29.21268516v1.full.
13. Fergus O'Sullivan, "The Pandemic Made Cities Quieter, But Not Less Stressful," *Bloomberg*, September 2, 2021, https://www.bloomberg.com/features/2021-Covid-city-noise/.
14. Francesco Aletta, Tin Oberman, Andrew Mitchell, Huan Tong, and Jian Kang, "Assessing the Changing Urban Sound Environment During the COVID-19 Lockdown Period Using Short-Term Acoustic Measurements," *Noise Mapping* 7 (August 7, 2020): 123–34, https://www.degruyter.com/document/doi/10.1515/noise-2020-0011/html?lang=en; and Simone Torresin, Rossano Albatici, Francesco Aletta, Francesco Babich, Tin Oberman, Agnieszka Elzbieta Stawinoga, and Jian Kang, "Indoor Soundscapes at Home During the COVID-19 Lockdown in London - Part I: Associations Between the Perception of the Acoustic Environment, Occupants' Activity and Well-Being," *Applied Acoustics* 183 (December 2021), https://www.sciencedirect.com/science/article/pii/S0003682X21003996.
15. Maanvi Singh, "Emboldened Wild Animals Venture into Locked-down Cities Worldwide," *The Guardian*, March 22, 2020, https://www.theguardian.com/world/2020/mar/22/animals-cities-coronavirus-lockdowns-deer-raccoons.

16. Francesco Salamone, Lorenzo Belussi, Ludovico Danza, and Italo Meroni, "A Survey-Based Approach Used to Analyse the Indoor Satisfaction and Productivity Level of User in Smart Working during Lock-down Due to the COVID-19 Pandemic," *Journal of Physics: Conference Series*, 2021, https://iopscience.iop.org/article/10.1088/1742-6596/2042/1/012139; and UNESCO, UNICEF, and World Bank, *The State of the Global Education Crisis: A Path to Recovery* (Paris: UNESCO; New York, UNICEF; Washington, DC, World Bank, 2021).

17. Ulrich Glogowsky, Emanuel Hansen, and Simeon Schächtele, "How Effective Are Social Distancing Policies? Evidence on the Fight against COVID-19," *PLOS ONE* 16 (September 22, 2021), https://journals.plos.org/plosone/article?id=10.1371/journal.pone.0257363.

18. Peter Daszak, C. Das Neves, J. Amuasi, D. Hayman, T. Kuiken, B. Roche, and C. Zambrana-Torrelio, *IPBES Workshop on Biodiversity and Pandemics* (Bonn, Germany: Intergovernmental Science-Policy Platform on Biodiversity and Ecosystem Services, 2020, https://ipbes.net/sites/default/files/2020-12/IPBES%20Workshop%20on%20Biodiversity%20and%20Pandemics%20Report_0.pdf.

19. Andrea Giglio, Ingrid Paoletti, and Maia Zheliazkova, "Performance-Based Design Approach for Tailored Acoustic Surfaces," *in Digital Transformation of the Design, Construction and Management Processes of the Built Environment*, eds. Bruno Daniotti, Marco Gianinetto, and Stefano Della Torre (New York: Springer, 2020), 137–48, https://link.springer.com/chapter/10.1007/978-3-030-33570-0_13; and Maia Zheliazkova, "An Integrated Computational Approach for the Design of Tailored Acoustic Surfaces," *Proceedings. Euronoise* (October 2021), http://www.sea-acustica.es/fileadmin/Madeira21/ID121.pdf.

20. "Köral," AntiCAD, accessed April 25, 2022, https://anticad.com/koral/.

21. Y. Liu, Z. Ning, Y. Chen, M. Guo, Y. Liu, N.K. Gali, L. Sun, Y. Duan, J. Cai, D. Westerdahl, "Aerodynamic Analysis of SARS-CoV-2 in Two Wuhan Hospitals," *Nature* 582 (April 27, 2020), https://www.nature.com/articles/s41586-020-2271-3; and L. Liao, W. Xiao, M. Zhao, X. Yu, H. Wang, Q. Wang, S. Chu, Y. Cui, "Can N95 Respirators Be Reused after Disinfection? How Many Times?" ACS Nano, May 5, 2020, https://pubs.acs.org/doi/10.1021/acsnano.0c03597.

22. C. Yeo, S. Kaushal, D. Yeo, "Enteric Involvement of Coronaviruses: is Faecal-Oral Transmission of SARS-CoV-2 Possible?" *Lancet Gastroenterol Hepatology*, April 2020, https://pubmed.ncbi.nlm.nih.gov/32087098/; and L. Yu, G. Peel, F. Cheema, W. Lawrence, N. Bukreyeva, C. Jinks, J. Peel, J. Peterson, S. Paessler, M. Hourani, Z. Ren, "Catching and Killing of Airborne SARS-CoV-2 to Control Spread of COVID-19 by a Heated Air Disinfection System," *Materials Today Physics*, December 2020, https://pubmed.ncbi.nlm.nih.gov/34173438/.

23. "U.S. Department of Labor's OSHA and CDC Issue Interim Guidance to Protect Workers in Meatpacking and Processing Industries," *Occupancy Safety and Health Administration*, April 26, 2020, https://www.osha.gov/news/newsreleases/national/04262020; and "Workplaces and Businesses," *Centers for Disease Control and Prevention*, October 18, 2020, https://www.cdc.gov/coronavirus/2019-ncov/community/organizations/meat-poultry-processing-workers-employers.html.

24. "Significant Events and Progress Involving the Meat and Poultry Industry during the COVID-19 Pandemic," *North American Meat Institute*, December 17, 2020, https://www.meatinstitute.org/ht/a/GetDocumentAction/i/179846.

25. Sigfried Giedion, *Mechanization Takes Command* (Minneapolis: University of Minnesota Press, 2013), 228–29.

26. Ibid., 101–6.

27. On representing labor in food infrastructure, see Meredith TenHoor, "Labor in the Logistical Drawing," *Log 34* (Spring/Summer 2015): 139–42.

Chapter Four

1. Stuart Butler and Carmen Diaz, "'Third Places' as Community Builders," *Brookings*, September 14, 2016, https://www.brookings.edu/blog/up-front/2016/09/14/third-places-as-community-builders/.

2. "Architectural Epidemiology," accessed April 25, 2022, https://www.architecturalepidemiology.org.

3. P. Emrath, "Higher Lumber Costs Add More than $35k to New Homes Prices, $119 to Monthly Rent," *Eyehousing*, 2021, https://eyehousing.org/2021/higher-lumber-costs more-than-35k-to-new-home-prices-add-119-to-monthly-rent.

4. Ibid.

5. Jen Miller, "Why Lumber Prices Are Spiking," *Supply Chain Dive*, May 27, 2021, https://www.supplychaindive.com/news/lumber-demand-shortage-price-saw-mill-board-housing-pandemic-labor/600876.

6. Sophie Mitchell, "What We Can Learn from the Spiking, and Tumbling, Price of Lumber," *Reuters*, August 25, 2021, https://reutersevents.com/supplychain/supply-chain/what-we-can-learn-from-spiking-and-tumbling-price-lumber; and Brendan Murray, "The Forgotten Shipping Pallet is Staging a Pandemic Era Rally," *Bloomberg Businessweek*, April 9, 2021, https://www.bloomberg.com/news/articles/2021-04-09/the-forgotten-shipping-pallet-is-staging-a-pandemic-era-rally.

7. Dmitry Ivanov and Alexandre Dolgui, "Viability of Intertwined Supply Networks: Extending the Supply Chain Resilience Angles Towards Survivability. A Position Paper Motivated by COVID-19 Outbreak," *International Journal of Production Research* 58 (April 15, 2020), https://www.tandfonline.com/doi/full/10.1080/00207543.2020.1750727.

8. Salomée Ruel, Jamal El Baz, Dmitry Ivanov, and Ajay Das, "Supply Chain Viability: Conceptualization, Measurement, and Nomological Validation," *Annals of Operations Research*, March 8, 2021, https://link.springer.com/article/10.1007/s10479-021-03974-9.

9. Maciel M Queiroz, Dmitry Ivanov, Alexandre Dolgui, and Samuel Fosso Wamba, "Impacts of Epidemic Outbreaks on Supply Chains: Mapping a Research Agenda amid the COVID-19 Pandemic through a Structured Literature Review," *Annals of Operations Research*, June 16, 2020, https://link.springer.com/article/10.1007/s10479-020-03685-7.

10. "The Nine Planetary Boundaries," *Stockholm Resilience Centre*, accessed April 25, 2022, https://www.stockholmresilience.org/research/planetary-boundaries/the-nine-planetary-boundaries.html.

11. Slavoj Zizek, "There Will be No Return to Normality after Covid. We Are Entering a Post-Human Era & Will Have to Invent a New Way of Life," *RT*, December 8, 2020, https://www.rt.com/op-ed/508940-normality-covid-pandemic-return/.

12. Edward T. Hall, *The Hidden Dimension* (New York: Anchor Books, 1966).

13. Quentin Meillassoux, *After Finitude: An Essay on the Necessity of Contingency*, trans. Ray Brassier (London: Continuum, 2010).

14. Guy Debord, *The Society of the Spectacle* (Paris: Buchet-Chastel, 1967).

15. Designed by OPEN Architecture, the Chapel of Sound is an open-air music hall situated within the mountainous terrain north of Beijing. The monolithic concrete construction resembles a massive, porous boulder, with an outdoor amphitheater and stage that are visually connected to a Ming Dynasty section of the Great Wall.

16. *See States of Entanglement: Data in the Irish Landscape*, ed. ANNEX (Barcelona: ACTAR, 2021) and Entanglement, the Irish Pavilion at the seventeenth Venice Architecture Biennale 2021, curated by ANNEX, https://entanglement.annex.ie.

17. Research toward this project is made possible by the SOM Foundation Research Prize in 2019 in affiliation with the School of Architecture at the University of Illinois at Chicago under the title "Hot Farms: How Emails Grow Tomatoes."

18. Timothy W. Luke, "Urbanism as Cyborganicity: Tracking the Materialities of the Anthropocene," *New Geographies: Grounding Urban Metabolism* 06 (Cambridge, MA: Harvard Universiy Graduate School of Design, 2014), 39–53.

19. See *Stay-at-home Stress: A Spatial Survey of Low-income Households in Houston's Fifth Ward during COVID-19*, accessed April 25, 2022, https://stayathomestress.com/. Funded by Rice University's COVID-19 Research Fund, the six-month pilot study was codesigned with Gabriel Vergara and undertaken with the assistance of graduate students Caroline Francis and Carrie Li, in correspondence with Leah Wolfthal, Elizabeth Silva, and Nikki Levigne at the Fifth Ward Center for Urban Transformation.

20. For a reflection on the role of qualitative research and drawing as a social record, see Amelyn Ng, "Stories from the Pandemic: A Spatial Survey of Stay-at-home Stress," *Journal of Architectural Education* 75, no. 2 (September 2021): 275–83.

21. See "Findings," in *Stay-at-home Stress*, accessed May 15, 2022, https://stayathomestress.com/Findings.

22. See Bruno Latour, "What Protective Measures Can You Think of So We Don't Go Back to the Pre-Crisis Production Model?" first published in *AOC*, March 29, 2020, https://aoc.media/opinion/2020/03/29/imaginer-les-gestes-barrieres-contre-le-retour-a-la-production-davant-crise/, accessed http://www.bruno-latour.fr/sites/default/files/downloads/P-202-AOC-ENGLISH_1.pdf.

23. Magda Mostafa, author of the *Autism ASPECTSS Design Index*, quoted by the authors.

24. Laura Parker, "How to Stop Discarded Face Masks From Polluting the Planet," *National Geographic*, April 14, 2021, https://www.nationalgeographic.com/environment/article/how-to-stop-discarded-face-masks-from-polluting-the-planet.

25. Anna Tsing, *The Mushroom at the End of the World: On the Possibility of Life in Capitalist Ruins* (Princeton, NJ: Princeton University Press, 2015).

26. Julia Blazy, "Polypropylene Fiber Reinforced Concrete and its Application in Creating Architectural Forms of Public Spaces," *Case Studies in Construction Materials* 14 (June 2021), https://doi.org/10.1016/j.cscm.2021.e00549.

27. Stanton M. Chapman, "New Mushrooms have been Discovered that Can Eat Plastic," *Fungal Futures*, March 15, 2020, http://www.fungal-futures.com/new-mushrooms-have-been-discovered-that-can-eat-plastic/.

28. Muhammad Haneef et al., "Advanced Materials from Fungal Mycelium: Fabrication and Tuning of Physical Properties," *Scientific Reports* 7 (January 24, 2017), https://www.nature.com/articles/srep41292.

Chapter Five

1. Iñaki Abalos and Juan Hereros, "Toyo Ito: Light Time," *El Croquis* 71 (1995), http://www.toyo-ito.co.jp/WWW/Book_Descript/1990-/1990-b-03/1990-b_3_en.html.

2. Toyo Ito, "Architecture in a Simulated City," *Oz* 14 (1992): 52, https://doi.org/10.4148/2378-5853.1237.

3. "Why Americans are Rethinking Where They Want to Live," *Economist*, December 18, 2021, https://www.economist.com/united-states/why-americans-are-rethinking-where-they-want-to-live/21806771.

4. Ibid.

5. Ibid.; and "The Great Pandemic Migration," *Wall Street Journal*, December 28, 2021, https://www.wsj.com/articles/Covid-states-migration-lockdowns-census-11640733268.

6. Joel Kotkin, "After Coronavirus, We Need to Rethink Densely Populated Cities," *Fortune*, April 1, 2020, https://fortune.com/2020/04/01/coronavirus-dense-cities-urban-rural/.

7. "Revisiting Frank Lloyd Wright's Vision for 'Broadacre City,'" *Frank Lloyd Wright Foundation*, September 8, 2017, https://franklloydwright.org/revisiting-frank-lloyd-wrights-vision-broadacre-city/.

8. David J. Peters, "Community Susceptibility and Resiliency to COVID-19 Across the Rural-Urban Continuum in the United States," *Journal of Rural Health* 36 (June 16, 2020): 446-456, https://onlinelibrary.wiley.com/doi/full/10.1111/jrh.12477.

9. Ibid.; and Ian F. Miller, Alexander D. Becker, Bryan T. Grenfell, and C. Jessica E. Metcalf, "Disease and Healthcare Burden of COVID-19 in the United States," *Nature Medicine* 26 (June 16, 2020), https://www.nature.com/articles/s41591-020-0952-y.

10. Edward Glaeser and David Cutler, *Survival of the City* (New York: Penguin Publishing Group, 2021), 23.

11. Cody Miller, "9 in 10 Seattle Residents Support Pandemic-era 'Streateries,' Survey Finds," *King5*, February 24, 2022, https://www.king5.com/article/news/local/seattle/streateries-outdoor-dining-survey/281-1cc81996-c418-4b70-beb0-5156d0bf2423.

12. Megan Maurer and Dan Poniachik, "City Parks: A Lifesaver During COVID Winter," *State of the Planet*, Columbia Climate School, November 12, 2020, https://news.climate.columbia.edu/2020/11/12/city-parks-Covid-winter/.

13. Kathleen McCormick, "Room to Roam," *Lincoln Institute of Land Policy*, October 7, 2020, https://www.lincolninst.edu/publications/articles/2020-10-room-roam-pandemic-urban-parks-what-comes-next.

14. Ibid.

15. Sheldon Cohen, William Doyle, David Skoner, Bruce Rabin, and Jack Gwaltney Jr, "Social Ties and Susceptibility to the Common Cold," *Journal of American Medical Association* (June 25, 1997), https://jamanetwork.com/journals/jama/article-abstract/417085.

16. Susan Pinker, *The Village Effect: How Face-to-Face Contact Can Make Us Healthier and Happier* (Toronto: Random House Canada, 2014), 67–68.

17. Damien Carrington, "Two-Hour 'Dose' of Nature Significantly Boosts Health–Study," *Guardian*, Jun. 13, 2019, https://www.theguardian.com/environment/2019/jun/13/two-hour-dose-nature-weekly-boosts-health-study-finds.

18. Joan Iverson Nassauer, "Messy Ecosystems, Orderly Frames," *Landscape Journal* 14, no. 2 (1995): 161–70, https://deepblue.lib.umich.edu/handle/2027.42/49351.

19. Mark Hostetler, "Cues to Care: Future Directions for Ecological Landscapes," *Urban Ecosystems* 24, no. 1 (June 5, 2020): 11–19, https://doi.org/10.1007/s11252-020-00990-8.

20. An example is the ancient Greek city of Priene, situated in Western Turkey, with a block size of 115 x 154 feet (35 x 47 meters). See "The Greek Grid Towns," *Quadraletics*, accessed April 25, 2022, https://quadralectics.wordpress.com/4-representation/4-1-form/4-1-3-design-in-city-building/4-1-3-4-the-grid-model/4-1-3-4-2-the-greek-grid-towns/.

21. Theo Deutinger, *The Pandemic Space* (Kassel, Germany: Kassel University Press, 2020).

22. Emil Kaufmann, "Three Revolutionary Architects: Boullée, Ledoux, and Lequeu," *Transactions of the*

American Philosophical Society (Philadelphia, PA: American Philosophical Society, 1952), https://hdl. handle.net/2027/uc1.c055305688; Peter Lang and William Menking, *Superstudio: Life Without Objects* (Milan, Italy: Skira Editore, 2003); Mark Nelson, "Some Ecological and Human Lessons of Biosphere 2," *European Journal of Ecology* 4, no. 1 (2018): 50–55, https://doi.org/10.2478/eje-2018-0006; Dror Poleg, *Rethinking Real Estate: A Roadmap to Technology's Impact on the World's Largest Asset Class* (Cham, Switzerland: Palgrave Macmillan, 2020); Ellen Vaughan and Jim Turner, "The Value and Impact of Building Codes" (Washington, D.C.: Environmental and Energy Study Institute, 2013), https://www.eesi. org/papers/view/the-value-and-impact-of-building-codes; and Ludger Hovestadt, Urs Hirschberg, and Oliver Fritz, *Atlas of Digital Architecture: Terminology, Concepts, Methods, Tools, Examples, Phenomena* (Basel, Switzerland: Birkhäuser, 2020).

23. Juan Prudente and Hackensack Meridian Health, "How to Create a Covid Bubble and Why You Should Consider One," *HealthU*, August 26, 2020, https://www.hackensackmeridianhealth.org/en/ HealthU/2020/08/26/how-to-create-a-Covid-bubble-and-why-you-should-consider-one#.YhsR4S-B1qt.

24. U.S. Centers for Disease Control and Prevention, "How to Protect Yourself and Others," accessed February 27, 2022, https://www.cdc.gov/ coronavirus/2019-ncov/prevent-getting-sick/ prevention.html.

25. Rachel Gutman, "Sorry to Burst Your Quarantine Bubble," *Atlantic*, November 30, 2020, https:// www.theatlantic.com/health/archive/2020/11/ pandemic-pod-bubble-concept-creep/617207/.

26. Doug Brugge et al., "Developing Community-Level Policy and Practice to Reduce Traffic-Related Air Pollution Exposure," *Environmental Justice* 8, no. 3 (2015): 95–104, https://doi.org/10.1089/ env.2015.0007.

27. American Institute of Architects, "COVID-19 Resources for Architects," October 28, 2021, https://www.aia.org/ pages/6280670-COVID-19-resources-for-architects.

28. Jenny Schuetz, "Rethinking Homeownership Incentives to Improve Household Financial Security and Shrink the Racial Wealth Gap," *Brooking's Blueprints for American Renewal and Prosperity* (Washington, DC: Brookings Institution, 2020), https://www.brookings.edu/research/rethinking-homeownership-incentives-to-improve-household-financial-security-and-shrink-the-racial-wealth-gap/;

Sebastian D. Romano et al., "Trends in Racial and Ethnic Disparities in COVID-19 Hospitalizations, by Region—United States, March–December 2020," *MMWR Morbidity and Mortality Weekly Report 70*, no. 15 (2021): 560–65, https://doi.org/10.15585/mmwr. mm7015e2; and Lauren M. Rossen et al., "Disparities in Excess Mortality Associated with COVID-19— United States, 2020," *MMWR Morbidity and Mortality Weekly Report* 70, no. 33 (2021): 1114–19, https://doi. org/10.15585/mmwr.mm7033a2.

29. William Combe, Pic Nic 1–14 (January 8, 1803– April 9, 1803) (London: R. Exton for J. F. Hughes, 1803).

30. Hannah Arendt, *The Human Condition* (Chicago, Illinois: University of Chicago Press, 1958), 52.

31. L. M. Sacasas, "Common Worlds, Common Sense, and the Digital Realm," *Convivial Society*, October 25, 2020, https://theconvivialsociety.substack. com/p/common-worlds-common-sense-and-the?s=r#details.

32. Arendt, *The Human Condition*, 52.

33. "Best of Boston 2020: The COVID-19 Heroes Edition," *Boston Magazine* (2020).

34. Erica Olson, Margaret Hansen, and Amber Vermeesch, "Mindfulness and Shinrin-Yoku: Potential for Physiological and Psychological Interventions during Uncertain Times," *International Journal of Environmental Research and Public Health* (December 14, 2010).

35. Alexander Gillis, "What is the Internet of Things (IoT)?" *TechTarget*, accessed April 25, 2022, https://www.techtarget.com/iotagenda/definition/ Internet-of-Things-IoT.

36. Paul Theerman, "From Central Park to the Front Lines: Frederick Law Olmsted and the Sanitary Commission," *New York History of Medicine & Public Health*, April 26, 2016, https://nyamcenterforhistory.org/2016/04/26/ from-central-park-to-the-front-lines-frederick-law-olmsted-and-the-sanitary-commission/.

37. Naomi Sachs, "Question for the Group: Are Healthcare Facilities Using Outdoor Spaces, Including Gardens, Differently Due to Coronavirus?" LinkedIn post, March 2020, https://www.linkedin.com/feed/update/ urn:li:activity:6646499732308938752.

38. Black Doctors COVID-19 Consortium, accessed April 25, 2022, https://blackdoctorsconsortium.com.

Index

Image Credits

Published by
Princeton Architectural Press
70 West 36th Street
New York, NY 10018
www.papress.com

Editors: Jennifer Thompson, Linda Lee
Designer: Paul Wagner

Library of Congress Cataloging-in-Publication Data
Names: Brownell, Blaine Erickson, 1970– editor.
Title: The pandemic effect : ninety experts on
    immunizing the built environment / Blaine
    Brownell.
Description: First edition. | New York : Princeton
    Architectural Press, [2022] | Includes
    bibliographical references and index. |
    Summary: "Leading architects, designers,
    materials scientists, and health officials reflect
    on the influence of COVID-19 on buildings and
    cities-and propose solutions to safeguard the
    built environment from future pandemics"—
    Provided by publisher.
Identifiers: LCCN 2022022410 |
    ISBN 9781648961649 (paperback) |
    ISBN 9781648961922 (ebook)
Subjects: LCSH: Architecture—Health aspects. |
    City planning—Health aspects. | Architecture—
    Human factors. | COVID-19 Pandemic,
    2020–
Classification: LCC RA566.7 .P36 2022 | DDC
    362.1/042—dc23/eng/20220617
LC record available at https://lccn.loc.
    gov/2022022410